GRUMPY IN SPAIN

By John. S. Moody

Copyright © 2016

All rights reserved.

ISBN-13: 978-1523422654
ISBN-10: 1523422653

Many thanks to

Judith Williams, for proof reading my efforts, and sticking with it.

To Spanish friends, Sergio and Maria for sorting out most of my problems, and being such good people.

Pen sketches by John Simpson Moody

To the fates that guided me to this fascinating country, which has so enriched my life.

Table of Contents

FORWORD 6
EXTRANJERO 11
MY FIRST HOME IN SPAIN 13
THE HOUSE FROM HELL, SITUATED IN PARADISE 16
THE LOCAL BAR 18
CHARACTERS 20
OLD CARS 26
KNOCKING THE BRITS 28
THE THREE TYPES 30
BLISS AND TORTURE 32
HEALTH COVER AND WORK 34
EVERYTHING IS DIFFICULT 36
THE LANGUAGE 39
THE FIESTA 43
THE MATANZA 49
QUEUING 53
CORRUPTION AND THE BACKHANDER 55
LOOKING UP 58
I HAVE TO ADMIT THAT I KNEW NOTHING ABOUT CAVE HOUSES BEFORE COMING TO SPAIN 60
CARS AND OTHER THINGS MOTORING 71
ATMOSPHERE AND HAUNTED 76
FILM CAREER 82
STEALING TILES DOESN'T PAY 86
HOUSES 98

SAD STATE OF AFFAIRS IN SPAIN	100
WORK ETHIC AND THE ROAD TO WHERE?	103
YO VIVO	109
THE POLICE	110
BLOWING MY OWN TRUMPET	113
WOODROT	117
FLAMENCO	122
OLIVES, ALMONDS, ADVOCADOS, CHIRIMOYA and WINE	124
Almonds	126
Advocados	127
Cherimoya	127
Wine	128
POST	131
MY CATS THINK THEY ARE DOGS	133
SPANISH EXERCISE	142
WILDLIFE	146
CREEPY CRAWLIES AND THINGS THAT BUZZ	148
CRUELTY	151
INFORMATION, NOISE AND TELLING THE TRUTH	154
DO YOU CHANGE?	158
AFTERTHOUGHTS	160

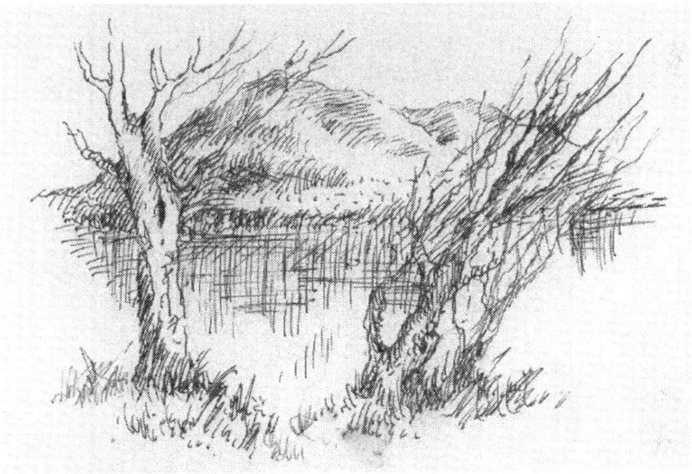

FORWORD

I was going to write a book about my fascinating and different experiences since moving to Spain, but then I thought 'Nah!' that's been done to death, and my friends out here would not read it, because to them, it's just everyday life. So what could I do? It took a while, but listening to two Brits sitting in a bar and complaining.

"Don't they know English is the universal language?"

It dawned on me, I could just as easily complain; I hope humorously about everything that, as a true Brit, I find difficult, bizarre, unfathomable, or just plain funny about living in another culture. That would be far more interesting, and fun to write about. Hence the title, **Grumpy in Spain**, was conceived. In the end I had to admit that unless I included the more interesting or downright nasty events I have been involved with, and even how I came to be here, then the book would be rather short. So now it is just as much a 'look at what I have done' book as any other. It is a complete mix, and would need a seriously good editor to sort it out. But what the heck, it was fun to write.

Most of the complaints in this book, and there are quite a few, are based solely on the fact that being English, I expect the rest of the world to toe the line and do everything the way that I would, although this is completely unrealistic, downright imperialistic, and in the end, the joke is on me. I also have to admit that in proofing and rewriting this book, I have added in just as many complaints about us lot, the British, as I have about the Spanish. I have tried not to be nasty, except in one chapter which will become obvious when you get to it.

You will find very little difference between large cities anywhere in Europe. Most of the big retail companies have their shops dotted all over the map, and there is always a MacDonald's just around the corner. Prices in Spain have been rising rapidly and luxury items are more or less on a par with Britain, although there are some anomalies. Second hand cars are very expensive here, even taking into account that they don't rust quite as much as those exposed to the British winter. But many things are still cheaper, and that is one of the reasons we all like living over here, and of course the sun.

If you want to experience the difference between the two cultures, then you have to live for at least a short while out in the campo, or one of the small villages, in my case within Andalucía, although I am sure that it is not so very different in other parts of this large country. You have to bear in mind that the population density is very low compared to England. Spain has forty seven million people with a density of about 91.4 people per square kilometre. England on the other hand is the most crowded country in Europe with 413 people per square kilometre. That is double the figures of Germany, and quadruple the figures for France. So why should I have complaints about a country, that gives me so much room to move about in, where things tend to be cheaper and where the sun almost always shines? Well as I said, I'm British so I have to complain about something!!!

Most people live around the coast or in the major cities, but large swathes of Spain are very thinly populated. The custom in the past was for the majority of a family to stay local, with only a few spreading their wings. However, the shortage of jobs and the new generations, who are not tied to the land like their fathers, has resulted in many seeking work abroad. The older generations kept stubbornly to their regional dialects, local traditions and attitudes towards how just about everything should be done, from the local Matanzas, meaning 'slaughter' or 'killing', to building houses that have little regard for weather conditions, but more on that later.

You would think that coming to live in the wilds of the Andalucían countryside, with not a neighbour in sight, and just enough money to keep body and soul together, that my life would be tranquil. It would be almost, but not quite boring, with the blazing heat radiating down, day after day. Well that's what I thought! Anyway seeing as it's actually pouring with rain, blowing a gale and decidedly cold, I may as well start this tale of my experiences in the 10 years I have been living here. I hope it is going to be a funny account of the idiosyncrasies that make the rural Spanish and British ex-pats such alien creatures to each other, seen through the eyes of someone, who thinks far too much for his own good. Although I often 'take the Michael', out of the way things are done here in Spain, I should like to make it clear that I have some very good, and extremely helpful Spanish friends, and for the most part, since living here have been treated with more generosity and kindness than I deserve. I just hope they don't read this book.

In England I got up each day, grabbed some breakfast and went to work, came home had my tea, did a bit of revision, watched TV and then went to bed. Friday night I had a couple of pints with my mates, and Saturday and Sunday were swallowed up doing house repairs, the garden, the car or watching more television , now that is what I call a boring life. I remember the last hour, the last minute, walking away from my final job. I was going to look back over my shoulder, but why? I didn't miss it; already it was being consigned to the past. The next two weeks were like bliss, getting up when I wanted, drifting around; it was definitely different than from being on holiday. Somehow it was a bit scary and open ended as if you had finally escaped from life's grind; it was almost, but not quite a guilty pleasure. Of course things were not going to last, at best I had a few months before needing a way to earn some money, but for then it was a good sensation.

For several years I had been going on about moving abroad, but it never got any further than talking. Then one day at a party, I had obviously been boring a friend about my intentions, when he stopped me in mid-sentence.

"Why don't you go and do it then, instead of just talking about it?"

He had a point, and after I had got down off my high horse, I agreed and started to set the wheels in motion. It took a year to clear and sell the house, search for a new home online and finally pack the car. That was over ten years ago now, and somehow I have managed to lead my own life, and not gone back to working a '9 to 5' or being at someone else's beck and call. I have never been on the dole and never done a day's work since, that I did not want to do. I cut expenses to a minimum, and never bought anything I didn't really need. I had got out of England to a much cheaper country, and lastly using my limited skills, worked for myself. This involved all sorts of odds and ends, jobs like helping friends build a holiday villa, looking after gardens and holiday homes for vacant tenants, selling and teaching art to adults, and writing online. This year I have reached my so called pension, so it seems like I've made it. Looking back to my tedious life in England

and comparing it to what has been accomplished since living here in the middle of nowhere, there is no comparison. I have written eight books, and appeared in a full length film. Then there was the Spanish marching band, over fifty of them, and me the only foreigner struggling to play the saxophone. More to my taste was the rock/folk band I played guitar with; that have performed at several bars and special fiestas. I have run several music events, called 'Woodrot' on my vacant land each May; the first was four years ago, it is small but fun. The second year we had six bands playing and over 300 people sitting on the sloping hill enjoying themselves. The third year we had a massive thunderstorm which rather altered events. Last year we held it in the local village.

I've had an exhibition of my paintings in a lovely old converted nunnery and am now living in a cave house, which I have slowly converted from a basic shell. On the less positive side, I've had a hernia operation, my knee replaced with a false one, and now recovering from a broken leg that required five screws and a plate to hold it together, silly bugger, I fell of a ladder!

So that's the potted history over with.

EXTRANJERO

The word basically means foreigner, and for anyone who has lived abroad in a country that requires you to learn another language to communicate, you will understand just how hard a sounding word that is.

I remember my first attempt at conversation with a Spaniard, it was in a petrol station and I was desperate for a wee, "Desperado PeePee", was all I could think to say. It was more successful than I expected, but that could have been because I had my legs crossed, and was adopting a slightly strained crouched position. He grunted and pointed to a block house at the end. Two minutes later I was back, still adopting the same posture and about to utter "necesitooo llave." But he beat me to it, for he was holding out the key on a length of string, with the biggest fob of wood on it I have ever seen. Hobbling back I glanced at it, in bold letters it said in Spanish, "Do not steal", (I had to look that up later, my Spanish wasn't that good yet.) On the same trip down I encountered a barman who was determined not to understand me; all I wanted was a cup of coffee. After I had pointed at the cup of the guy next to me, he proceeded to grin at his mates and ask me what type of coffee I wanted, reeling off a whole load of options, and knowing full well I was stumped. I was going to walk out, however I decided not to let him win, so I just smiled and asked if he spoke Spanish! When you realise that this is Andalucía, and thus the regional accent is much like Cornish is dissimilar to a BBC accent, you realise what a good insult I had come up with. It wiped the supercilious grin off his face, and then I walked out. It was at that point I realised I could survive in this new, exciting, but at that time, alien environment.

Apart from the obvious problems of buying even a loaf of bread, completing an official form, making your requests or intentions known, there is a bigger problem. We just don't do things the same way! It's like coming at every single attitude and belief, every course of action, from a different set of rules, learnt from birth. This may be difficult to understand, but if you read the next couple of chapters, it may start to make some sense.

Being British it comes hard to consider yourself a foreigner, it is supposed to be those other people who come from abroad that are aliens. Even on our annual holiday to Benidorm, or some such mass appeal beach, the average person from the UK does not think of themselves as Foreign. Mind you, as just about every bar in these places, has all day fried breakfast, fish and chips and English speaking waiters, it's not so surprising. You would be hard pressed to find someone speaking Spanish; the predominant accent seems to be something north of Birmingham. (England, not Alabama)

Our other big problem is that the English language has spread so far that we have become very lazy, and expect everyone to speak it. So come the day that you decide to up sticks and live abroad, the tables are quickly turned and it is not long, about five minutes, before you realise that you haven't a clue about almost everything. You are the stranger, and you had better start getting used to it.

MY FIRST HOME IN SPAIN

The mule stood in the road, a saggy old beast. The cut esparto grass bundled on its back stuck out at least a meter either side of its flanks. The form of a small Spanish local was perched somewhere amongst it, engaged in a heated discussion with the driver of a car that blocked the remaining space in the road going through the village. I sat patiently; this was normal up here in the hills of Andalucía. I once read somewhere, that by law they could have five minutes before you had any right to complain. I think that was just someone being sarcastic.

Andalucía is in Southern Spain and approaching its rich fertile plains from the north is like entering another world. My first sight of this lush land that the Moors loved, was akin to seeing a fantasy dream, the shimmering heat, blue hazy mountains and olive green countryside stretching out before me. The dusty plains of La Mancha, home of Don Quijote (or Quixote, if you prefer) and Sancho Panza, that I had travelled through, were a stark contrast. I will never forget those moments before I moved on down into my new life. Starting all over again after a series of disasters, my whole life packed into the back and on top of an old estate car, it felt like being reborn. Of course such moments don't last and reality soon re-asserted itself, but I am getting ahead of myself.

Ben, the son of the man selling me my house was standing outside when I pulled up for the first time. He was short and swarthy with a terrifyingly firm handshake as befits someone who was a blacksmith by trade. I once saw him walking down the street with a steel girder on his back. Later, I tried to lift just one end off the floor, and couldn't. I was to see him regularly, as unknown to me the house I had purchased included a cellar that was not mentioned in the deeds, this turned out to be his workroom. Now I realised why it had been so cheap. A friend of mine who suffers from tinnitus once told me that the brain eventually trains itself to ignore continuous noise. It took me two years to ignore the intermittent hammering on steel from below. Ben was considerate in his own way; he would shout up that he was going to make some noise; it was a signal for me to head for the local Bar. We got on well and shared a few beers over the next five years. He helped me settle in, sort out where to buy things for the house and introduced me to Megas de Pan, one of the most boring foods you could wish to find. His mother once forced me to eat two bowls, of what were basically fried breadcrumbs with, if you were lucky, a very rare bit of fried fish. I was gagging long before I had consumed several glasses of her homemade wine to wash it down, after that everything was a bit of a blur.

I had driven down through Spain with two beds and a sofa strapped to the roof rack of my car, there was so much stuff on top that I was extremely lucky not to get stopped by the Guardia, something that has happened several times since. It seemed like half the village came out to look at me struggling in with all my things, apart from Ben nobody offered to help. He told me later that because my car was so overloaded they thought I was Rumanian. (I guess that they had a particular thing against them.)

I also learnt quite quickly that it was quite normal to stare at people, or the driver of every car that goes past. In fact if they didn't stare at you as you drove past, it was a bit of an insult, as if you were not worth staring at.

Although the village was dirty and noisy, (because every other man was a self-taught builder, with his own dumper truck,) it was situated in the most wonderful mountain valley with beautiful views all around. The sub-tropical climate encouraged the plentiful orange and lemon trees, and avocados grew bigger than a boxer's fist. Just the shortest walk from your front door and you were in the Garden of Eden, Cherimoyas, almond and pomegranates added to the profusion of wonderful smells.

I suspect that many of the locals had no way to judge how beautiful it was, especially to someone who had lived in a city. They took it for granted, and even built the local waste dump right in front of what I considered the best view of the valley.

The smallholders would take their crops of olives and avocados down to the co-operative warehouse, they would be paid by the going rate, or have their olives ground and be given back, as olive oil. At the height of the season, there was such a surfeit of produce, that if you mentioned you liked fruit, the next day there would be carrier bags full of lemons and oranges hanging from your front door handle. A word of advice, don't ever offer to help with picking any crop with your friendly Spanish neighbours. Slapping down olives and hauling them away in nets is backbreaking work and seems to go on for days. The trees vanish into the distance in endless rows, and you never seem to get to the end. Unless you are really fit and healthy, or have done it all your life, steer clear. Avocadoes are a little easier, but you will be swinging precariously from very thin branches trying to grasp bunches that are just out of reach. Don't ever consider lettuce, unless you never want to stand upright again.

THE HOUSE FROM HELL, SITUATED IN PARADISE

With such idyllic surroundings I suppose there had to be a downside. Unfortunately, my new home that I had only previously seen in photographs had more drawbacks than just having a blacksmith in the cellar. It looked great from the outside, with three levels leading to a veranda and courtyard on the roof. The views out of the back, over the valley were incredible, the best view, was when sitting on the loo! The large window was not frosted, but nobody could look in, as it was a shear drop of thirty foot outside. The problem was that all the windows howled and rattled every time the wind blew, the outside walls were only one brick thick, so inside, it was boiling in summer and freezing in winter. Judging by the iron rings set in the wall, I think it had once been used for housing animals rather than people; it may even have been a slaughter house, back in its dim distant past. They just didn't do double glazing or central heating in these villages. Added to this, on the opposite side from the views, the house was built into the side of the road, so every car that passed made the house rumble. As there was a car every few minutes, not to mention vans and dumper trucks, it was quite a combination, together with the howling wind, rattling windows and the blacksmith hammering. Needless to say my trips to the bar increased, only stumbling home drunk when all the workforce had decide to head to the same bar. Even then due to the lack of sound proofing, I would lay awake until 2am, listening to the old ladies who would sit outside my neighbour's house nattering incessantly. Often they were talking about me, but my Spanish was then not good enough to understand most of it.

My village was 10 kilometres up a winding road with several steep drops on either side, until you crested the rise and saw the green valley spread out below you. The village was one of three that were fairly close together. One was quiet with tiny little narrow streets, the other was pretty and multi-cultural, the third was noisy, dusty and always full of cement piles and stacks of bricks, and yes that was the one I ended up in! However despite its problems, it was on reflection the best one for me. Of the other two, Gujar Alto considered itself more cosmopolitan, it had a worldly air, it physically and I think mentally looked down on the other two villages. Quite a few of its residents had actually travelled abroad, not sure why some of them came back. Poor Danny had made it to a big city before returning and getting trapped running the local shop, he often moaned about almost escaping.

I liked Gujar Fondon, it really felt like going back in time. But in a way it had become so relaxed, it was almost asleep. It is only a guess, but I bet a lot of the older residents had never been further than the local town for supplies. It felt like you could drift the rest of your life away, but maybe that would have been too dangerous for me.

My village, Gujar Faraguit may have been scruffy and noisy, but it was very much alive. Most locals were very protective of their own village at the expense of opinions about the residents of the other two. It always made for plenty of amusing and disrespectful comments in the bar.

THE LOCAL BAR

In an effort to integrate myself into the life of the village, I attended the local bar, far too often during my first year. My intake of alcohol shot up alarmingly. Likewise what had been the occasional cigarette turned into a thirty a day habit. They gave you one, you gave them one back, so then they gave you another and so on indefinitely. As initially my Spanish was so bad, it helped over the pauses between trying to communicate, until we all got too drunk to care. My home was in a direct line down the road from the bar and on a clear day it would take me ten minutes walking, but after a few too many, it would take more like an hour. On one occasion, I headed off in the wrong direction and ended up in a maze of little streets. Confronted by a solid wall at the end of a particularly difficult set of turns and twists, I sat down on someone's doorstep and fell asleep. An hour or so later a nice old lady fed me very strong black coffee, and made her son usher me back to my own doorstep. A few days later and totally sober I tried to find the house again in order to thank her, but after two fruitless hours I gave up looking. Drunkenness does not have much of a social stigma in those parts; it was far too common, with very little employment and far too much time to fill under the hot sun. Some of the older men arrived at the bar at 6am when it opened for their coffee laced with rum, and did not leave till it closed its doors at about one the following morning. You will be glad to hear that I hardly touch a drop now and have given up smoking completely. It dawned on me one day that I was so desperate to be accepted, that I was doing things and associating with people, which I would never have contemplated back in England. It was not me and it had to change. Funny thing is that I wheeze much more now that I don't smoke, but someone said it is because cigarettes deaden the follicles in the bronchial tube, so they don't react. So if you need an excuse to keep smoking, I have just given you one, it stops you wheezing.

I don't seem to have enough hours in the day to do all the things I want to do, but looking back to that first year or so, I don't remember doing much at all except hanging around and drifting through the day. I can see now, how a lot of the older men in particular, had accepted this as the norm, and found no problem with doing very little. The life of a small village up in the hills was very different from the bustling town just a half hour drive away. It would have been very easy for me to become accustomed to that way of life, after all who hasn't dreamed of getting away from modern life and all its stresses?

On the surface most of these men seemed quite content and mentally balanced. However this was not always the case, and the more you learnt about them and their past, the more obvious it became that there were deep rooted issues. But I guess that's the same for us all, you can go to the furthest corner of the earth, but you can never get away from yourself, and I was starting to find that out.

CHARACTERS

It quickly became known, that the Englishman at the end of the village was an artist, and it was not very long before the other artists came to check the competition out. The first was Alonso; he appeared on a decrepit old motorbike and shook my hand vigorously, before glancing around in nervous agitation. He became a good friend in time, but he had many problems including being Bipolar and having a compulsive disorder, that could only be coped with by painting pictures, at a faster rate than Van Gogh! His little studio was stacked from wall to wall with canvasses. To be honest they were naive, often rushed and very childlike, but from time to time he would produce something that contained a rare charm and power of its own. He also did wood carvings from tree trunks that reminded you of the Easter Island sculptures. I liked these better and have one in my studio. Unfortunately the wood has some kind of parasite living in it, and if you listen quietly you can hear it gnawing away. From time to time a small hole appears and there is a little pile of sawdust on the table, but once the thing reaches air, it must turn around and head in another direction. One day the whole sculpture will just fall apart. (I have since cut away almost all of the wood, it is now just a mask, but I never found the creature, however all is silent.)

Alonso would stay for only a few minutes each visit, try to sell you a painting and then head for the next port of call, which was usually a bar. He never stayed any place for more than a short while, so spent his day rushing from one bar to another, unless he was working feverishly in his studio. His medication had to be adjusted carefully, otherwise things got out of hand, and one day he drove around completely naked. Another time he appeared with his hair styled like Elvis Presley and wearing a hideously garish Hawaiian shirt, luckily it was a small village and everyone knew his problems. From time to time he was taken into a secure unit in Granada to sort out his medication. I really liked Alonso He was nice and kind, but a lost soul who eventually succumbed to his condition and departed for a better world.

Juan was a small wiry figure, gaunt, serious and someone who really did look like a haunted artist, he was always smart, but his clothes were old, he reminded me of Quentin Crisp. You could well imagine that he lived on absinthe and scraps of food, whilst painting his dark dream tortured canvases. The problem was that he always tried to involve me in some scheme or other, usually something to do with going drinking in some far off village bar high in the mountains, for which he needed me to drive him. On the first couple of occasions I spend hours watching him slide slowly under some table or other, and on one trip, we did not get home for two days, so in the end I got very adept at spotting him coming and dodging out of sight. He called me the Grey Fox, not sure why, because I had brown hair at that time, and he was continuously complimenting me on my art and referring to me as the maestro, usually in an effort to get another lift somewhere. Four years later I went back to the village after moving away, sadly to find that both of my competitors had died, mostly from their own lifestyles. It made me sad, but relieved that I was not the tortured artist type, just someone who likes painting.

   Maybe it was because it was a small community, where everyone knew each other and many generations of families had been born, grown up and married locally, sometimes never leaving the area, that it seemed to have more than its fair share of strange people, not always in a bad way.

Characters proliferated, and Manuel was one of them. He turned up outside my door one day on a Harley Davidson copy. Revving like mad to get my attention, he thrust five litres of homemade wine into my hand and proceeded to follow me into my kitchen. Bearing in mind I had never spoken to the guy before, it was a little unnerving. We shared a couple of glasses at 9am in the morning. It was powerful stuff and I could feel my head starting to get befuddled. Then he slapped me hard on the back and was gone in a puff of exhaust fumes. The guy had style; he looked like a poor version of Charles Bronson, and was very proud of his moustache. I met him often after that and never saw him sober, except on one occasion when he reverted from talking his usual gibberish into quite an interesting and knowledgeable man. It was a pity that drink ruled his life; he did not have a job but was pensioned off from the Guardia on health grounds. Two incidents in particular make him stand out as a character. Somehow one day he managed to drive a dumper truck off the side of the mountain. It crashed down several hundred feet. He jumped off at the last moment and knocked himself out when his head hit a rock. Later in hospital with a large dent in his forehead, he awoke to find several tubes and sensors attached to his body. Ripping them all off, he walked 15 kilometres home from the hospital, because he thought he would have to pay for treatment. On another occasion he trapped his father and his dad's new girlfriend in their house, by firing a shotgun at their front door. He thought that as the woman did not like him, his dad would rule him out of his inheritance. He got arrested and found himself in jail for several months. Unfortunately in jail he got dried out, but on the first weekend that he was allowed out, he overdid it and promptly died.

Paco at the bar worked all the hours that God gave, but he was always on top of it, chatting and keeping the endless customers happy. One of his sons was extremely fat and would sweat profusely whilst working behind the bar. The son was not a good looking person, and I always wondered how he managed to have such a stunning girlfriend. One day he was riding a rather small scooter, over a mountain pass, when he managed to leave the road and disappear down into a gully that he could not get out of due to his unfit condition. Apparently he was down there six hours before someone heard him pressing his horn and flashing his lights. Last time I returned to the village to visit old friends I found that his father, Paco had suffered a stroke and was confined to a wheelchair unable to talk. All that hard work, for so many years, and for what? He remembered me smiled and muttered my name, it brought tears to my eyes and even now, while I am writing this. I told the old owner of the bar I now use near my new home, about Paco. His name is also Paco, and he also works very long hours, and only has two weeks holiday a year visiting family. I said that he has plenty of money and should take time off and use some of it to enjoy himself, before it was too late. His reply was that he had always worked in the bar, and would not know what to do with time off.

In my present village there is a guy that you would swear was a poet. He always dresses in strange combinations of clothes. One day it will be a Cossack hat, white dinner jacket with turned up collar and trainers. The next day it will be a cowboy hat, Etonian tie and jacket and calf length stitched boots. We always have a short chat, mostly because he is trying to tap me for a euro, but I don't mind because he is a character and goes his own way. I was told a story that one of the rich Spanish landowners, paid him to sit all night in an empty cave with a dead donkey. It was like holding a wake for the animal. Apparently two hours of sitting there with flickering candles in a cave, staring at the dead animal was enough and he fled the scene.

The local goat herder was a short fat man with ample chest hair which jutted out between the buttons of his shirt. He either had numerous shirts of the same colour and pattern, or it was the same shirt he used for three years. I never saw his home, but the locals said that he slept with his animals in their pen. The time he proposed marriage to Rebecca was surreal to say the least. Rebecca was at least a foot taller, twenty years younger, smartly dressed and a highly intelligent New Zealand woman. He ambled up, pulled out two 50 Euro notes from his pocket and pronounced his love, adding that he had money to keep her in the custom she expected, and that he would give up living with the animals. Well! Something like that, as he was generally rather drunk most of the time.

I don't know if it's the sun, Latin blood, small tight knit communities, but this part of Spain sure has a lot of characters. Thinking back to cold, damp Britain, I don't remember meeting many genuinely crazy characters. (In the best sense of the word.) In the case of the goat herder, I wish I had some of his confidence, to face the world and see it as I want, rather than as it is. But that seems to be a common trait with the rural Spanish from these small villages. I am not sure that many of them have experienced alternative ways of doing anything, they are so confident in what they think they know, and consider the rest of us are wrong, certainly they think most foreigners are stupid. Any suggestion that something could be done a better or more efficient way is instantly ruled out, they really do not like change, from what their predecessors did. This may sound a rather opinionated and generalised statement, but ask any extranjero, or for that matter any Spaniard who has travelled, or lived abroad, and they would tend to agree with me.

OLD CARS

Eventually my old Volvo estate that had carried me and my only worldly goods all the way to Spain, gave up the ghost. It had done well climbing up steep rutted tracks for a year or so. But finally it ground to a halt high up in the hills on a bit of wild land I had purchased for a song, because it was so inaccessible and could not be built on. The view was fantastic; my village was just a tiny cluster of colour way below. I had intentions of constructing an overnight shed that I could escape to in order to contemplate life from time to time, and get away from the hammering of the blacksmith in my cellar. The last load of planking, cement bags and blocks had been too much for the old girl. As no breakdown service in the entire world was ever going to come and sort me out, I pushed her under an olive tree and there she is today, some eleven years later. I don't live in this area anymore and only visit rarely, a bad injury to my leg precludes me walking up there, and I would not attempt it in any half decent car, but I can still just see her with a pair of powerful binoculars. I am glad she did not end up on a scrap heap in North London; this is a much more dignified way to rust, sunning herself under the Spanish sky.

Her replacement was a little white van, the sort that they use to go around the villages selling fish, fruit, veg and even cement. Basic functional ability, no air conditioning or much in the way of springs for that matter. It only lasted a year, and then one day it just burst into flames. Within thirty seconds it was full of white billowing smoke. The dog and I escaped and then stood around with several locals watching it burn. One of them made the joke that fires were not allowed during the summer months, but I didn't find it that funny. One of the most frightening experiences was being towed back down the mountain road, by a Spanish friend who must have forgotten that I was on a short bit of rope. Although the car was partly burnt out, the brakes still worked, but I had only fractions of a second to react, as he was belting along. I was just beginning to get the hang of it when we met the local bus coming up the hill, at a point that was not only a curve, but on a bridge with stone walls each side. How I got through the gap with my eyes firmly shut, I will never know. The local policeman kindly arranged to have it towed away for free, after it had sat outside my house for two months. Despite the village being a bit of an eyesore, apparently a burnt out wreck was too much even for them.

KNOCKING THE BRITS

Nothing in this book is in order. I have been in Spain now for over twelve years, and I can't believe how the time has flown. Instead of working my way through a timeline, I prefer to jump around and pick whatever I choose to illustrate my tirade of abuse at a country and people that I have actually become very fond of.

Now for another little knock at us British, who choose to come out here to live a new life. There is very little logic in upping sticks and moving to another country, especially one that does not speak your language. Having spent most of their life in the comfort of a culture that they understand, people then throw themselves into a daily nightmare of complete frustration, and more than a bit of blind panic. Nothing works as they expect it to, and many after a year or so return home, often minus the funds they went out with. You get people suddenly deciding that running a bed and breakfast in Benidorm would be a great idea, it looks interesting on the TV, in programmes such as 'A Place in the Sun' or 'How to waste your entire life savings' (made that one up, as if you didn't guess.) They put a deposit on a villa that is being built (supposedly) It will have five bedrooms a sun lounge and swimming pool and only be five minutes' walk from the beach. What they may actually have, is a set of dubious plans from a developer, who gave a backhander to the outgoing Mayor, for permission to build on restricted land. Somewhere there will be a pile of sand, some cement bags that have gone hard, on an unfinished road that is actually four miles from a beach, that is next to a landfill site. I only wish that I was exaggerating. Spain went barmy building; it used more cement than any other European country, in the hope that it could build its way out of recession. (Well actually they never realised there was a recession, or pretended not to notice.) There are hundreds of half completed complexes lying empty, and developers that can no longer be found. A national paper did a survey of local authorities who are now being prosecuted for misdealing. Apparently the courts will be busy for years. They showed a map of Spain with little flags in it to denote corrupt councils; the map was covered in them. What is really sad for some ex British is that they moved into completed dwellings, only to see them bulldozed down because they were illegal, and these people got very little, or no compensation.

Don't get me wrong, I am not looking down on anyone that wants to start a new life in another country, I can hardly criticise, after all that is exactly what I have done. Perhaps I was just lucky, certainly I did not plan things carefully, being a romantic, I just set forth on an adventure. (Sounds better than saying I was too dumb to organise anything). My first purchase was at least 100 years old and in the middle of a village, so hardly likely to be illegal or pulled down, and the cave house I now live in is over 250 years old, and hasn't fallen in yet. I didn't plough all my savings into a dream, because I didn't have any savings anyway. I didn't drag dependents with me, and have no intention of returning to England unless I am physically dragged or kicked out of Spain for being responsible for the Armada.

You have to go with the flow when living in another country, forget what you expect and concentrate on what happens.

THE THREE TYPES

Driving over Lemons by Chris Stewart started the ball rolling for many Brits who wanted to get out of the rat race and get back to basics. Many followed suit, some succeeded and some went home after realising just how hard it is to start again, especially in a country where you don't speak the language, have no idea of how anything is achieved or don't understand the character of the Spanish way of life. The Extranjeros (Foreigners) that's us, sort of split into three basic types. Chris Stewart lived near a town called Orchiva, back then it was quiet, but is now full of what we called hippies, but are now apparently called Crusties or New Age Travellers. They live in an assortment of homemade geodesic domes, tents, wigwams, and rough huts on the mountainside around that area. I once gave one of them a lift back from the coast and was given a guided tour of their enchanted hillside. I suppose when you are 19 and trying to find yourself, but still have your parent's spare credit card concealed in your bed roll, then it's an interesting experience. But it seemed to me that an awful lot of them were over fifty, and had somehow lost their way in life.

Then there are the gated communities on the coast, spending their time playing golf, mat bowls and bridge. For men, it is obligatory to wear shorts, and black socks with sandals, not a good look. All the women seem to have white hair and tans that are natural, but look fake, because they are so brown. The last few pages of any local free paper would always have images of the mixed four pairs, over seventies annual bowls winners, or the British production of songs from the Sound of Music, by the local coffee morning club. Couples appear to be retired, and thus quite a lot of them, particularly the men ,die out here. There was an estate near where I used to live, that was nicknamed Widows Hill. These ladies often found themselves stranded and alone, no happy retirement for them.

Then there are the rest of us scattered widely throughout the countryside and small pueblos, trying to live amongst what we like to think of as, the locals. We generally purchase a rundown village house, cortijo, farmhouse, or even in my case a cave house. The next few years are spent trying to reform our individual piles of rubble, and believing we are builders, even if the previous forty years were spent behind some desk in a nameless office. We keep all the local builders merchants in business, by buying three bags of cement and thirty cement blocks at a time, then wonder why our car suspension collapses. Most of us were never built for heavy labour at the arse end of our years, but think it will be cheaper than hiring a local builder. Speaking personally the effort has totally wrecked my body, so when I eventually sit down in my rocking chair, having completed every reform , I hope I have enough time left to look around and appreciate what I've achieved, before I nod off for good. Mind you it is not permissible to stop, especially with a cave house. Close a door, walk away and when you return something has happened, even if it is only a layer of dust. A section of ceiling fell out a few weeks ago and landed at my feet. It is then that you remember that there is thirty foot of earth above you. At least if it collapses it will save on my funeral expenses, I will already be buried.

BLISS AND TORTURE

My first year or so was a complex mixture of bliss and torture. It was a far cry from overcast Northampton, and the prospect of teaching in noisy schools till I was old and grey. To end up in such a beautiful and warm place that had only seen snow once in thirty years, yet with problems, I could do little about. I knew that I would have to change, but the crazy existence was so intoxicating that somehow I lasted over three years, before I finally did move, to my present cave house home. In retrospect it was a good thing. About a year after I had left, there was a major land slip, my ex-property being only one brick thick, decided to split into two separate houses. On the roof terrace you had to take a leap of faith to reach the other part. I feel very sorry and not a little guilty for the people who purchased it from me; I was not to know what would happen. I hope they had good house insurance. I recently returned to see a few old friends and was gladdened to see that the house had undergone serious structural repair, and was once again looking one solid residence. Whilst I lived in that area I took several jobs that came my way. One of them was to tend the gardens and make sure the houses stayed in good shape for foreign owners that could only come over from time to time. One such place was a beautiful mill house that had been around for perhaps two hundred years, in one form or another. It was now fully converted and being let out as a holiday home. My job was to keep the swimming pool clean and get locals in to clean the house, and wash bedding between guests. I also had to meet and greet new holiday makers and give them all the help I could. Being nice and sociable, I not only got paid for doing that, but the guests usually invited me around for meals and brought me more than the occasional drink. One of the perks of the job was that they usually over stocked the fridge, and on leaving for their flights home, would ask me to see if anyone would like three bottles of wine, whisky, ham, cheese and god knows what else. Obviously I duly obliged. This way every couple of weeks my own fridge would fill up with all sorts of goodies. On the rare occasion a party would eat up all their remaining supplies, it was very disappointing.

 Anyway I was talking about this mill. It lay low down in the river gorge, but there had never been any problems, until we had a mighty storm. Unfortunately they had been dramatically changing the water channel further up the valley; this had caused a funnel effect. The storm only lasted a few hours, but the sheer volume of water took down trees and washed away tons of earth. It poured down the gully, and all but took the mill with it. The swimming pool filled up with solid mud, and all of the downstairs was at least a foot deep in evil smelling earth. A hire car was washed away downstream, this time luckily no one was inside the house. It took me two weeks to dig the swimming pool out with a spade, as it was impossible to get a digger near enough. The insurance finally paid the owners and the place was re-formed with new barriers to stop it happening again. Unfortunately almost a year later another storm hit, causing even worst damage. The entire swimming pool broke up and was washed away. Downstairs, the doors had all been busted in and a tree was actually in the living room. It was enough for the owners, who walked away from a 400,000 euro home. I am not sure, but I think the insurance company refused to pay the second time.

HEALTH COVER AND WORK

Most Brits come over with a temporary international health card E111. This is fine if you are on holiday, it will cover you, should you be unfortunate to fall ill or have an accident. However it is not enough if you choose to live here. Becoming a full Spanish citizen takes several years but you can apply for residency and also a health card. There are pros and cons to the citizenship, but the health card is more or less essential. Unfortunately you have to waive your rights to British health care, which many are loath to do, in case they want to go back. Getting to see the local doctor is difficult without a card. It may not be impossible, but you normally have to fight your way past a stroppy enquires and bookings desk. The card will link to all your medical history, and the doctor is less keen to be helpful, unless they have that to hand. The Rumanians and Peruvians seem to be able to get a card easier than us, but then I think it has something to do with the fact that they are willing to bend double and pick lettuce for nine hours a day in the hot sun, and we are not. If you work for a company out here they will have a health scheme system, but to get cover as a self-employed person you will have to pay Social Security each month, and that is not cheap. I think it is something over 200 euros per person, at the moment. My friend who suffers from stiffening of the joints needed special medicine that cost some 400 euro each time. He and his partner had to be self-employed and paying into the system, to be able to get the stuff. I know a few who are self-employed, but there are so few jobs in Andalucía, that I only know personally of one single Brit, that works for a Spanish company over here.

A lot of the Spanish around here don't work within the system, but make enough money to survive, by doing whatever job comes along. Mostly they are builders or work in some form or other on the land. They don't pay tax if they can help it. One particular guy in my last village actually made the vault gates for the local bank, and also the police station cells and they paid him in cash, which I know was never declared by either side.

It is hard here in the Campo; high unemployment means that if there is a way to milk the system it will be done. High numbers of ex-officials, particularly police seem to be pensioned off early with stress related problems. It's funny that quite a few seem to be able to hold down a job, selling bread out the back of a van or doing building work, or in the case of one man I know running a successful bar, chicken farm, and still have time to do odd jobs with his dumper truck. Staying in family units with several devious incomes coming into the home, plus selling an odd ruin to an unsuspecting Brit, has seen them accrue quite nice pension pots. I don't blame them; it's all part of the backhanded economy they grew up in. No wonder there is so much corruption in high levels of Government over here; they are just taking their natural skills to a higher level.

EVERYTHING IS DIFFICULT

Apart from the language, living in a foreign country, especially outside of the big cities is a complete cultural change. Nothing is the same. At first going into a shop needs courage and conviction that you can cope with asking for what you want. So, outside you practice the phrase for "can I have a loaf of bread?" That's all very well but when they then reply with

 "Do you want the wholemeal or plain white, and is that sliced or whole, or would you prefer a French stick or we have some nice granary baps?" you stand there with your mouth open, or utter a frightened "Si".

Filling in forms is a nightmare. For a start they use official language which tends to be nothing like everyday speech. In Andalucía they have not got over the habit of having everything in triplicate and stapled together. This will allow you to wait three months for a certificate which will prompt you to visit two offices, who send you to a bank to pay 7 euros and return with a slip, which they will then photocopy another three times. This will further allow you to apply for a permit, and so on and on. I wish that I could still find it, but there was a brilliant sketch by Spanish actors, where an office full of jobsworths, were frustrating the hell out of a woman client. The final scene straight out of a Clint Eastwood movie saw the man behind the desk and the lady hurling themselves towards the only staple gun in the room.

To tell you what I had to do, to just change the name of ownership on a car, would take up the whole page. Being stubborn I refused to pay an Abogado (Lawyer) like everyone else, but not next time.

It is amazing that anything actually gets done officially. I believe they have a secret system in all corridors of power from the local council office upwards. Everything does eventually happen if you are prepared to wait months, or bang on the counter enough times. I should just like to point out that despite six requests directly to the Mayor and his Technico sidekick, I am still waiting for a rubbish bin after fifteen months, since having two stolen in quick succession, just thought I would get that one in. Apparently all of them at the town hall are scared of the guy who drives the rubbish truck; he is some sort of Spanish Mafiosi who controls all the bins. He is so fat that he can hardly climb in and out of the cab, I would wave him down and complain, but I think he would most likely run me over. A friend of mine, who worked with him for a short while, said that he had complained that the Englishman sold his two bins, so he was not getting any more. Exactly how and why I would try to sell two worn out old plastic bins was never discussed.

Something may only take ten minutes or two years and there is normally no explanation as to which or why. It may get done at your first visit, but more normally requires two languages, ten phone calls, several letters and more than a few visits to different departments. You need the ability to accept the look of effrontery you will receive, if you try to suggest any inefficiency on their part. It is more likely that complaining (It seems to work for the locals) will only have the effect of increasing your waiting time.

Nothing is done in what we would consider a logical way. Obviously, it is us that have to adjust, after all we chose to come and live here. But you can't help thinking that there must be a reason why they make everything so complicated. The only answers I can come up with are that they have come a long way in a short time since the days of Franco. Everything is changing fast, but they are not a nation that likes to abandon their culture for progress, but naturally they want both. Almost daily rules are changing, yet archaic systems cannot be updated that quickly. Hence offices full of paper, which still has precedence over the flashy new computer systems, on which they generally can't find anything when you ask. It is also evident that with so few jobs available, everyone is making themselves indispensible. The more convoluted the system, the more someone is needed to work it. It is a case of Jobs for life, not many look for alternative employment.

I have to point out that I am referring to this part of Spain. If you go to Cataluña you will find that they consider Andalucía to be somewhat primitive. Cataluña believes that most of the country's wealth is generated by them and syphoned off by the Government to give to the rest. Hence the recent surge of enthusiasm to become Independent. At the time of writing, unlike Scotland, they are prevented from voting for freedom from the rest of Spain.

THE LANGUAGE

Down here at the southern end of the country, it is still hard to find anyone who speaks English. Many have a smattering of words but even most doctors, lawyers and local council officials do not speak anything but Spanish. In Britain it is much the same, we keep to our native tongue, but Europe needs English for commerce, the internet and as a common language. Most children have lessons and if you talk to anyone they always say that it is important if the country is to be part of Europe. I am not saying this out of laziness to learn Spanish; we should all make it a priority, seeing as it is now our home. But until you have been here a couple of years, it is an uphill struggle. The kids don't seem to have much of a problem, within six months they are chatting merrily away to their new Spanish friends; it's just us old codgers who have the trouble. One funny side effect I have noticed is that most Spanish have been raised on western pop music; they love all the same stuff that we grew up on. They can sing the words to Bohemian Rhapsody and Honky Tonk Woman, as well as anyone, but most still haven't a clue what the words mean. If you turn on a radio, it is always British and American music. I tried to imagine what it would be like back home in England, if every song I heard was in Spanish.

I was useless at French and German when at school, so it was no surprise to me that I have struggled to learn Spanish. It is not the basic words, but the sentence construction. Everything feels back to front, the object coming before the description. We say big house, they say house big. They have fourteen verb tenses, so that the endings of every verb are changed depending on whether it is past, future, present, past perfect subjunctive, and all the rest, you get the idea. There are over 1,100 verbs that apparently can all be conjugated, whatever that means, actually I know, but it's far too boring to explain. Add to that, are you saying, I, you, they, us, etc. actually most of the locals don't use all fourteen anyway, more like three or four of them. But then comes the problem of regional differences. Much like I haven't a clue what someone with a broad Manchester accent is on about, the Spanish have the same problem. The first thing that goes locally, is the ending of the words, and that is the part that tells you what the heck they are talking about.

Gated British communities on the coast, hardly make local contact. One lady I spoke to had been here for 16 years and still only knew a handful of words. That is actually disgraceful, but I can understand it is hard, I live amongst the local Spanish and still struggle to comprehend them. I was wondering why I have a particular problem with reading the Spanish newspapers, and then it dawned on me that it is all in the past tense, when we normally speak in the present tense. The main problem with the Brits is that we are remarkably stubborn about learning another language. Most of us had to do a bit of German or French at school, but I can't remember any of it now.

Still it gives my Spanish friends something to laugh about when I struggle to explain something. It tends to be a mixture of mime, individual words and a lot of puzzled looks. The mother of one friend had promised to make me some curtains, when I offered to pay her, my friend grew angry. The words 'Pagar' and 'Pago' mean very different things. I had offered to punch his mother, rather than give her a payment.

To express yourself, and be understood in a strange new language is almost magical when it happens. Your body assumes new positions, arms wave in exaggerated gestures and you find yourself patting and hugging people far more. Your facial muscles assume mime artist expressions; suddenly you are no longer plain John, but Juan or even Don Juan. I hate formal lessons, and this is coming from an ex-teacher. Sitting at an evening class, behind an old school desk that is three sizes too small for you, listening to someone rattling on about past participles, whatever they are. My neighbour agrees and say's "if you want to learn Spanish, talk to a Spaniard." He suggested we went to local bars, but I think he had an ulterior motive. However I tried it on my own, in order to save money on buying him, and his mates loads of drinks. At first when you walk in they all stare at you, but I am fast getting used to that, it is nothing personal. But once you can strike up some kind of conversation with one, they will all chip in with advice. I found the best ploy was to ask the barman a question, something like, "Do you know where I can buy building materials without being over charged, because I am a foreigner?" that sets up at least two different conversations, one about where to go and another about the politics of overcharging the innocent. One tip, never enquire about the price of a property from the owner, send in a local Spanish friend, the difference in price will be big. Normally, you will stagger from the bar two hours later, head spinning from contradictory information, only half of which you understand, and a bit lighter in the wallet because you still had to buy everyone a drink. Another tip I was given, if you want to escape from the bar before the intake of alcohol and Spanish words becomes too much, is to tell them you have to go to work. Tell them you need the money to support your family. They will not try to stop you because if there are two things that are important out here, it is work and family.

The next morning write everything down that you remember and look up how to spell the words. Then go to a builder's merchant and throw a few of the technical words at the person behind the counter. They will not dare to overcharge you because you now have the inside information.

Plaza Mayor, Baza

THE FIESTA

It is generally assumed by people who are suffering cold, grey miserable weather in whatever country they reside, that us lot in Spain are always on holiday. It is true that the sun shines a lot especially down here in the south, and that it does appear that there are a lot of religious, national and regional days off work. At the last count, each municipality can arrange fourteen public holidays per year. Nine are decided by the government, two by the local council and the others by the regional powers. The local ones are normally linked to the Saints days of which just about every locality has their own. If unfortunately one of the nine Government days falls on a Sunday, they just let the locals choose another day, after all who wants to lose a day.

The national holidays normally mean that literally everything shuts down, except a few enterprising corner shops that do a roaring trade in milk, bread, beer and general eatables that people forgot to stock up on. Even a lot of the bars close, along with banks, and supermarkets. But museums stay open and so do tourist attractions, if there is money to be made. The roads to the coast can get very blocked and popular beaches that are empty one day are suddenly heaving with near naked bodies. In August, which is more or less a full public holiday, it is surprising that the country does not tip over, as the interior cities empty and half the population head for the coast.

Being very cunning, they leave holiday days where they are if they fall midweek, rather than shifting them alongside a weekend to make it longer. This then allows for extra days to be sneaked in as recovery days. They are called "Puente Days" (Bridge days), thus creating a possible four day weekend.

Cultural differences are obvious in the numerous Fiestas that proliferate across Spain. Every little pueblo seems to have a special day, and if they can get away with it, extended to two or three or more days. The British tend to want to be in bed as soon after midnight as possible. However the Spanish do not suffer with that hang-up. Given half a chance, they start late and carry on till dawn.

They love processions, marching bands, solemn lines on Day of the Dead, fireworks and any chance to dress up. Each village has its Saint, and I doubt there is a day on the calendar that isn't dedicated to one of them. My local town puts on a show, where the Moors and Christians enact a battle involving a fake cannon that makes a loud bang, and ejects a cloud of confetti. They rush at each other with brave shouts, and then proceed to try and avoid actually being injured, except the few at the front who start to believe that they are actually in a battle.

There are rows of marching locals dressed in a mixture of costumes, some resembling Romans and Moorish fighters, but others seem to be more flights of fancy than historically correct. There is the cross between Robin Hood and Puss in boots, with large plumes, or the ones that think they are barbarian hordes. Ladies go to extremes and often dress up prams and infants in similar styles to their chosen costume design. Pity about the ever present sunglasses, wristwatches, and the odd mobile phone. It seems each set consists of about twenty people who spend a fortune on their costumes, and must form some kind of a private club. Setting up base camp in a local venue, they all proceed to have a great time, normally including serious alcohol abuse, over the fiesta period. Many of these groups appear to travel around more than one fiesta, makes you wonder when they have time to work. Some of the bigger towns even include prancing horses, chariots and on certain religious events there have been known to be crucified Christ's, using real people. My favourite are the Paco's, they dress simply in a Moroccan smock with a fez. Their job is to act drunk and march in an exaggerated stagger, but all in unison. Not easy to do when sober, even more so by the end of the day when many of them are actually four sheets to the wind. Some of the Paco's are young children who ape the stagger of their older brethren very well.

Over the years traditions have developed in individual towns. These vary from simply throwing water, flour or wine over everyone as they run down the High street, to the more colourful, tomato hurling. Vast quantities are used each August in Buñol in Valencia. It started years ago when young boys got into a quarrel at the Giants and Big-Heads parade and started throwing tomatoes at each other after a lorry overturned. These days over 150.000 tomatoes (40 metric tons) are ruined, before fire hoses wash the people down. Some 50,000 tourists turn up to watch and because they can't get out of the way, end up participating. Shopkeepers and homeowners have large plastic awnings to drape over their property. Interestingly the streets are really clean the following week, due to the acidity of the juice disinfecting the cobblestones.

Two of my local towns have what is called the Cascamoras, where they fight for possession of a statue of the Virgin de la Piedad. Roughly translated as, The Virgin of the Head (snigger). The story goes that a land worker called Cascamoras found the statue in a field near Baza and tried to take it back to his village of Guadix. However the locals apprehended him, considering it a sacred theft. As soon as the people in Guadix heard that their man had been foiled, they responded by attacking those in Baza. This is what they celebrate each year, by running through the town covered in black engine oil. However I believe it has now been replaced with synthetic black paint, in response to environmental and health issues.

The Fallas in Valencia in honour of the patron saint of carpenters, has twenty or thirty foot high characters made out of cardboard, wood, polystyrene and paper Mache. Whole groups of designers spend months creating them. Usually they are cruel lampoons of well-known celebrities or politicians. There is plenty of marching up and down, bands, and fireworks, which escalates into a night of mayhem when these sculptures often stuffed with fireworks are set on fire. The noise is so loud that the ground usually shakes, and it is seriously advised that pregnant women stay away.

There are many weird and wonderful traditions throughout Spain, but these are some of the most unusual that I have heard of, involving sardines, snails, rats, ants and jumping over babies.

The sardine Festival in Murcia is actually about burning a giant mock-up of a sardine. It started back in 1850 when a group of students held a meeting presided over by a sardine, symbolising fasting and abstinence after several days of partying. The testament of the lady of the sardine, Donna Sardine (Mrs Sardine) is read out from the balcony of the town hall, which is generally a humorous look at politics and local issues. The next day is a procession with giant paper Mache heads and brass bands. It is so popular that they even have the Sardine Appreciation Association with its own Brass band. Manned floats dedicated to the Gods of Olympus, scatter toys into the crowd and it all ends up with fireworks and bonfires and an awful lot of drinking. The funniest sight is of numerous ladies all dressed in mourning black with big white handkerchiefs, dabbing their eyes and wailing, but at the same time grinning from ear to ear as the sardine meets its fiery end.

The oddly named Fiesta of near Death Experiences occurs in Neves in Galicia. Participants pay respects to Santa Marta in gratitude for allowing them to avoid death, after a close encounter. They are carried around in coffins by their family and friends, during some very bizarre processions.

The snail festival takes place in Lleida. During the three days of eating, some 12 tons of snails are consumed. Now you would think that this fiesta had limited appeal, but some 200,000 visitors seem to suggest and digest otherwise. It is arranged by the snail club who has the grand title of La Federacio de Colles de l'Aplee Del Caragol. Eating snails obviously gives you a lot of strength, because they also like making human towers, where people climb on each other's shoulders, upward until the whole thing collapses.

 In the town of El Puig, at the fiesta of San Pedro Nolasco, they throw rats at each other. I assume they are dead ones, but as I don't intend going to see, you can look up the details yourself if you are so inclined.

In Laza in Galicia, they go out and find ants, or more to the point rather vicious termites. They roll them into mud balls, run back to town and throw them at each other. I presume they spend the rest of the night rubbing in ointment and getting drunk to ease the pain.

I'm really surprised that this last one is allowed on safety grounds, but in Castillo de Murcia near Burgos, babies in swaddling clothes are laid out on mats, for grown men in bright yellow costumes to jump over. The men are supposed to represent devils and the act of jumping over the infants, is meant to cleanse them of all evil doing. Apparently if the child misses receiving this so called protection, it will spend its life looking over its shoulder and waiting for bad things to happen. Although there is a get out clause, in which, as an adult they can go to Granada and jump through fire at the Hogueras festival. Let's get this clear, we are not talking about hopping over one baby, they are often in groups of six, and the men have no doubt been previously in the bar. It reminds me of Evil Knievel, leaping over buses on his motorbike.

THE MATANZA

This next part you may want to skip if you are delicate about raw meat and especially if you are vegetarian. The Matanzas is not just a day when they kill one or more pigs, for the yearly supply of meat, but it is also considered a celebration. Neighbours will gather together to kill, cut and preserve all the pig meat they will require. Chorizos and Salchichon (forms of sausage) are seasoned and stuffed and then hung to smoke for at least a month. The legs are cured for up to two years and the pig faces are salted and stored. Andalucía produces what is considered the choicest pig, called Ibericos, because these pigs eat a type of delicious acorn that is only found in this region.

Although the families do all the hard work, normally a professional is brought in to kill and cut up the main carcass. First the head is cut off, and the brain the size of a large walnut is removed. Next the ribs and loins and any parts that will remain as large sections are cured in salt for fifteen days or so, or sometimes frozen. The rest is attacked by the local women with vicious looking filet knives. They separate the meat from the many layers of fat. Salchichon is made with the lean scraps and blended with seasonings. Chorizo goes through a longer process, where more of the fat is used and ground in water with salt, garlic and paprika, before being forced into intestines and hung to smoke.

If you have never been to a Matanzas, be prepared if you get invited. If you faint they will most likely drag you into a corner and leave you. It is a full on day or more of, chopping, grinding and stuffing of raw meat. Women up to their elbows in blood and intestines laugh and joke, and round off each day with plenty of food and drink.

We are so used to buying our meat, all nicely packaged, I am not sure we even consider that it was just a short while ago, running around in a field. (If it was lucky.) I have no intention of taking part in a Matanzas, although I have been invited once or twice, but appreciate that they are doing, what we are not prepared to do.

Food is something I expected most of Europe to be better at than Britain. You see all these adverts of healthy people with baskets of fresh vegetables, or sitting at long wooden tables under the olive trees, the sun is shining down ,kids frolic around whilst everyone is tucking into mounds of cooked meats and large woven baskets of cut homemade bread. The wine is flowing freely and everyone is happy and laughing. Would someone kindly tell me where exactly this place is, because it sure isn't around here? Yes they have fine hams and tasty meats ,but they don't seem to do anything with them except slice bits and stick them on a plate with a bit of cheese and a cut tomato. Most bars have very similar menus and you can more or less guess what is on them, the same old, lomo and chips, or chuletas, or really depressing pizza. Actually I quite like a good pizza, but not when I want some tasty Spanish food. I am sure some of the older ladies cook really interesting meals in their homes, but I don't get that sort of invitation. There was a bar up in the hills near where I used to live that did a tasty Cocido (stew) it came in a big serving bowl and you helped yourself. It was pointless asking what was in it, because the answer would have been 'Everything'. When your ladle was withdrawn from the bowl it could have any sort of meat on it, all at the same time. On one occasion I scooped out a lump that looked decidedly like sheep's brains. I can be a bit squeamish, but had to admit that the flavours in their soups were fantastic. Actually it is an insult to call them soups, they were more like stews. They also gave you carafes of the second best wine I have ever tasted in Spain There is nothing to compare where I live now, unless someone knows something I don't. I don't even want to talk about Gazpacho, soup is meant to be hot not cold. As for Migas, why don't they just call it what it is, fried bread. Paella may be interesting the first few times you try it, but it becomes a bit boring after a while, after all it is basically just yellow rice with some bits added. The only thing that is good is tapas, at least it is still free (or almost) down in these parts, and a tasty morsel with each beer goes down well. If you are a heavy drinker, you have had a full meal by the end. A good bar will vary each tapa you get, although some think they can get away with dumping some already handled peanuts, or a few cheap dry crisps on you. Don't make the mistake of ordering a full plate of a particular tapa you liked, it never tastes as good for some reason. Taking your time, whilst you down your drink, somehow makes every little mouthful more exquisite. Watching people, who realise that the neighbour in the bar is not going to eat their tapa, is quite amusing. Timing is everything if you are going to beat someone else to the draw. In most parts of Spain you now have to pay for Tapa, once upon a time it was always free. Actually it is a great attraction, I have often gone for a drink more to get the tapa than because I was thirsty. There are different explanations as to how it all started. My favourite is the piece of stale bread they placed over the glass of beer to stop the flies nose-diving into the glass. Unfortunately the old men in the bar kept eating the bread and demanding another. Actually I have just been told by a friend that there are some good places to eat in this area that produce quality meals. However as the starting prices seem to be quadruple what I would expect to pay for a decent meal, they will not be getting my trade.

I so missed good food, that at one point I convinced myself that I would open my own bar in my present cave house. Unfortunately I am a lousy cook, so would have to hire someone local to do it, then try to teach them how to make roast beef and Yorkshire puddings.

Local Goat Man

QUEUING

The traditional Andalucían, is not especially fond of queuing. It does not matter if you have been waiting twenty minutes in the shop to be served, or even in the waiting room at the doctors. The moment the opportunity arises they are straight in there. On arrival it is customary to announce that you are there in a loud voice, just in case anyone would be mistaken that you do not need instant service. I have to say that it is normally the older generation, and more often than not those of the female variety. As most of them are less than five foot tall and I am over six foot, they just don't see me. I can be standing quietly right next to them and they are totally unaware. In fact I have lost count of the number of times older Spanish women have walked straight into me. Now I have time normally, and am prepared to wait if it is urgent, but then you have to listen to ten minutes of their talk about ailments or grandchildren with the person behind the counter, who even knowing that you were there first, proceeds to decide who they will and will not serve. On that point it has only been the emergence of customer service practiced by the big supermarkets that has changed grudgingly, the attitude of many shop owners. The idea that you actually need a bit of politeness, and some help with finding what you came in for instead of a grunt, a no, or even being ignored, whilst they do something that to you does not look that urgent, or important, or even worse are on a phone talking to a friend. The funny thing is that after five minutes standing there like an idiot, you mutter something derogatory and turn on your heels to leave. At that precise moment they ask you what you want. Depending on my mood or urgency, I either tell them that they have just lost a customer, or I buckle in and politely ask for what it was I was hoping to get a few minutes earlier.

Another aspect that I noticed early on was that you will rarely hear a Spanish person in a shop or bar say "Thank you." Not only that, but asking politely with a please is often absent. It is more likely to be "Dar mi" (Give me) or! Quiero una" (I want one) or "Escucha mi" (listen to me). If you say thank you, it may be returned with a "no pasana" (It passes nothing) or "y tu" (you too) they are more likely to wonder why you are saying thank you, when you are going to be paying for it anyway. We see it as rudeness, but obviously they don't. I struggled to understand how they could be so blunt, until a local Spanish lawyer summed it up for me. He said "Well what do you say when you really mean thank you, when you are genuinely grateful, if you use it all the time for trivial things."

Because we were brought up to be polite, well some of us, we tend to over use thank you, hence the nickname that the Brits have acquired. We are referred to as 'Los Por favores.'

 Whilst on the moan, why is it that people don't seem to realise that they actually have to pay for things, until the person behind the counter asks for it. Watching people fumbling around in over stuffed handbags or through ten different pockets, trying to pay by picking out all the fluff covered loose change, before realising that it is not enough and then producing a high denomination note that will fill their pockets with even more change, is very frustrating. What about the person who brings back one pair of cheap pants to the supermarket, because they are the wrong size. Don't they know how big their backside is? Whilst twelve other people wait with their weeks shopping, this person is busily ratifying their exchange of purchase with the cashier. Let's face it, the waist band is too tight, because you ate too much sodding ham and cheese.

CORRUPTION AND THE BACKHANDER

As Spain struggles to change a system of corruption that actually worked quite well in the past, many councils and government officials and mayors are being prosecuted.

In a country where bribes, backhanders, doing favours, illegal building and ignoring regulations was almost the norm, it has caused a storm of protest from its citizens who are struggling in this economic climate, whilst high ranking officials are pocketing small fortunes. At the time of writing this part (Nov 2014) the present Prime Minister Mariano Rahoy, who has not been without controversy himself, tried to downplay the problem in his country. Shortly after, fifty one officials, bureaucrats and business leaders were arrested in wide ranging corruption charges. Some of these actually belonged to his own Peoples Party. Most were to do with granting of illegal contracts, money laundering and embezzlement, worth roughly £197 million pounds in the last two years alone. Bear in mind, this was an investigation in just one part of the country, around Madrid. There seemed to be an awful lot of Swiss bank accounts involved. Before a lot of this blew up I read a report that said it would take three years to process through the courts existing corruption charges, I suspect the figure is easily double that now. As an after note, I have just read that they have now arrested another seventy or so. I can't wait for the time they start looking into the police force themselves, that will be fun.

One of the big recent scandals involved the miss-use of company credit cards connected to the savings bank Caja Madrid. Including 1,500 euros spent by one employee at Ice cream shops. The bank became BANKIA which folded some two years later and forced Spain to apply for an E.U. bailout.

Even certain members of the Royal family of Spain have been implicating in corruption scandals.

At the moment the tide is turning towards a backlash vote at the next elections, PODEMOS a new party championing anti-austerity and promising to rid corruption, seems to be gaining quick popularity. But we have seen this all before, only time will tell. Normally good intentions and popular ideas are just not workable in the political arena. The country has over six million people unemployed and 150,000 families have been evicted from their homes in the last five years. Spain's fragile economy may not be able to withstand major political change.

Although corruption can never be excused, it is fairly normal human nature. On a small scale most of us do it, ask yourself, do you declare everything for your tax assessment, what about the cash payment for that little job at the weekend? Spain thrived on a system that everyone understood. Bartering is as old as the hills, I guess some people steeped in this method, were quite surprised that this way of coping, could be considered immoral or illegal.

Until very recently it was customary to pay a portion of black money when purchasing a property in Spain. This was to avoid paying excessive tax. The system was so ingrained that the lawyers would handle the transactions, often passing large wads of money between people in the adjacent office, or even the toilet in my case. The big problem for people who purchased under this system, is that the gap between the purchasing price on paper and what they actually paid, was in some cases extremely large. When they came to sell under the new tight regulations the capital gains appeared big when in fact it wasn't. An example would be if I purchased a property for one hundred thousand euros, but on paper it was sold to me for only forty thousand, and I gave the other sixty in black money. The seller would pay a lot less tax. But when I tried to sell it today for one hundred and twenty thousand, it would look like I was in line for eighty thousand euros profit, instead of the reality of a profit of twenty thousand, hence I'm not moving.

Despite legal battles being fought by organisations set up to help homeowners who were duped into buying illegal properties, the Junta de Andalucía regional government continue to demolish homes that are deemed unlawful. They are in part responsible for allowing, or at least turning a blind eye in the past to these buildings. We are not talking a few hundred, but many hundreds of thousands of so called illegal homes throughout Spain. The past corruption of builders, land owners and local council members has led to this situation, where innocent families have purchased in good faith and believed their documents to be legitimate. Particularly badly hit have been the British who assumed that the local planning laws were being followed when they purchased through supposedly legitimate sellers, using registered Abogados (Lawyers)

Church Baza

LOOKING UP

Ok time to lighten up for a moment. There are times in what should not now be a hectic day for me out here in the Campo (countryside), when I find myself with ten minutes and nothing to do, or more precisely, worry about. At moments like this the world comes into focus and you start to see what is actually in front of you. In my case, standing in my front courtyard looking over dusty olive trees, now barren after giving another healthy crop to the farmer. The silver grey and green leaves rustling in the slight breeze, the men have finished pruning the branches and re-fertilizing the land and now all is peaceful. The sun is already hot and it is only 10 in the morning and still only March. This winter has been dryer than most. Today, whilst it is cold and snowy in more northern climes, it is so warm, that had we been in England, it would be in all the papers about saving water. The distant blue misty mountains, their slopes covered in the distinctive striped pattern of more olive groves, make me realise just how lucky I am to be living here.

My friend has a wonderful ramshackle garden near Barcelona. It verges on an overgrown wood and consists of random metal and wood garden furniture that look like they have been there since the turn of the century. There are little shady corners and assorted planters full of strange spikey plants. The grass grows where it will and you can settle back, close your eyes and listen to the sounds of birds and the rustle of animals in the woods. At night you could be visited by the giant wild habalees (Pigs) that roam free. I have sat looking down on them from an open window just feet above, families snuffling around looking for food. They can be dangerous if confronted, but leave them in peace and they are magnificent creatures to watch.

During the day three ancient dogs and several cats laze in the sun and in the distance the sound of horses wandering the woodland trails.

Why is it we spend most of our lives worrying about things, never looking up at all the good things around us? An old cat with rheumy eyes and runny nose who suffers with stiff joints, is busy rubbing its body in rapture against an old tree stump next to me. It is oblivious to its problems, except the sheer pleasure it is now experiencing. My old dog that has trouble walking and is slowly grinding to halt, is stood listening to the country sounds around it, he hasn't moved for five minutes. Think I will do the same, time to put down the notebook and pencil and relax. Bugger! they have decided that my country lane needs resurfacing; the quiet peace was shattered at about 5am this morning. I have watched this process on other roads near here and know what I am in for. Firstly without telling the local populous they start really early and rip up the old tarmac with a dirty great bull dozer. This leaves a jumbled mess that looks like the surface of the moon. No car can get over it, so they then think its ok to leave it like that over the weekend. Any trip you want to make, assuming you can actually leave your premises will have to entail a long circular route across the campo. They never put the road closed signs at the junctions. They put them a few yards down the lane from where they are working. This means that unsuspecting motorists have to turn around and go back after travelling several kilometres down an eventually blocked road. Next will come lorry after lorry of sand, equally impossible to drive over, I know I once got stuck between several of these monsters, and was glared at for trying to attempt the impossible. Lastly comes the fiery tarmac machine, but because it comes from a different company we may have had to wait two weeks for its arrival.

I HAVE TO ADMIT THAT I KNEW NOTHING ABOUT CAVE HOUSES BEFORE COMING TO SPAIN

The day came when enough was enough with my first home in Spain. Too small, too hot in summer, too cold in winter, too noisy, too near the bar for my own good, and no garden for the animals. I started to look on the internet. In all I probably weaned it down to about fifty possibilities, some of the places looked fantastic, but after visiting half a dozen that were in the locality, I realised just how fanciful estate agents blurbs can be. One place was superb inside, but the view outside was row upon row of plastic greenhouses. They obviously had not shown them in the photo, or mentioned their existence. I find that really annoying, especially if you have come a long way. Another had a good view of the municipal rubbish tip. One said easy access, but they failed to mention that it was almost at the top of a mountain, along a road that you would certainly not want to travel along on a daily basis. One fantastic place was like a hidden village deep in a valley between towering mountains. The path down to it was just gravel; you took your life in your hands driving down to it. It was the sort of place that you would only come out of once a week to get shopping and probably not at all in the winter. Another old stone barn, had arched windows and rustic balconies, it looked on the internet like a stone version of an alpine cabin. This one turned out to be on the main trunk road to Madrid. I looked up as far as Cataluña and across to Extremadura in the west. There was a lovely smallholding with ancient olive trees, so broad you could not get your arms even a quarter of the way round the trunks. It had a stone barn, but no water or electricity. Another place offered you the whole valley as far as you could see and a ruin to reform. I had some great daydreams about how I was going to change some of these places. I could cope with living very basically; I think that was what I was secretly looking for all the time anyway.

I was driving around looking for a new place to live, having found a really nice lake, my friend and I stopped for a coffee at a thermal baths that nestled on the edge of the water. It was rustic and the bath area was a curved channel that ran around part of the café. It reminded me of a Roman bath house. Apparently when the council had decided to flood the valley, by building a damn, the local farmers were compensated. This chap had decided to use the naturally warm waters coming off our local mountain, to create this place and provide himself with a steady income. When we left I took a wrong turning trying to cross the valley and after descending we came across an old iron bridge leading to a dirt track. It looked far too dodgy to cross so we decided to turn around. However before we departed, I looked at the houses that perched on the slope on the other side of the small river and commented that they looked really interesting and that was the sort of place I would like to live. We then doubled back and found our way north. Months later when I finally settled in my new home, I went for a walk, with the distinct impression that I had been here before. All my previous approaches had been via the local village and along a tarmac road, I had never ventured down the unmade track going the other way. Suddenly I came across the old metal bridge from the other side. Tuning around I saw the same view I had witnessed months before with my friend. Without knowing it I had purchased the very same home that I had seen and liked on that trip. The metal bridge had seemed on the point of collapse, and that was back some seven years ago, is still there and used every day by tractors, cars and the odd adventurous lorry. I have always thought that it was intended for me to find this place, but may be that is just wistful fantasy.

I had never considered a cave house, the ones I had seen in Guadix looked unexciting, flat frontages set into dark cliff faces, but the advert said it had five bedrooms, large living room, overlooked fertile valley, and came with an awful lot of land. There was also a stone cottage joining it all, for the price of a one bedroom flat in England. As we drove up along a dirt path, the estate agent spread his arms wide and said this is all your land if you buy. Having only had a small terraced garden in England and none at all in my previous Spanish house, it was just too much of a temptation. But then I saw the building, well from that angle it looked like a dilapidated small stone building with the roof caving in, it was not inspiring and my heart sank again. Then we turned a corner and entered the front yard. It became clear that the bit I had first seen was just an outbuilding, what now presented itself was a three sided building that looked immense. The view over the valley to a distant lake and a majestic mountain was perfect. When he told me it had mains water and electricity, I was in love.

The cave house that I now live in has been around for at least two hundred years and must have quite a story to tell. Although you cannot see the light from any other dwelling as it is way out in the country, I have never felt the least bit apprehensive living here alone. It has an honest earthy feel about it; once upon a time families and their animals occupied these rooms. It was a hard life working the land, but they shared a common existence. Once numerous people lived near here, now there are just a handful of us new generation settlers. I must have known that cave houses existed, but assumed that they were dark and tunnel like; well the tunnel bit is not far from the truth. Nearby Guadix boasts the impressive district named "Barrio Troglodyte". In a way I am quite proud now of being an official Troglodyte. Ever since the Moorish occupation of Andalucía, the idea of living underground to escape the intense heat of summer has been popular. Even forty years ago, many of the now abandoned caves were lived in. Although in recent years local Spanish especially the young have opted for more modern housing, they have been replaced by an influx of foreigners like myself, who find the whole idea of being under thirty foot of earth rather appealing. The small settlement around me once had over two hundred souls living here, now it has about twenty five and fourteen of those are foreigners.

The rock is a mix around here of sedimentary limestone with layers of harder horizontal rock which was impervious to water. Digging out the softer layers allowed you to pull down the harder ones.

Originally the caves had no front other than a door and one or two windows carved out by hand. There would be an entrance tunnel, high enough to walk in. branching out from this would be further carved out rooms for the family and all the animals. If you needed more space you just kept digging. There is an old tale that when a wife knew she was pregnant, her first task was to start digging a bedroom for the baby.

When I first moved in, I had to duck down through every doorway, although the actual rooms where high enough for my six foot frame. It goes to show how in just two generations, the local Spanish have shot up in average height. If you look at the little old ladies and bow legged old men, you get an impression of how tough life must have been, with little money and a poor health system. Other advantages of owning a cave home include no roof repair bills and few external walls to keep in good condition. Heating bills are not generally anything like those of my previous homes and I don't have interfering neighbours. The arrangement of rooms would depend on the structure of the hill and individual requirements. Some dwellings had more than one entrance or even went right through, and out the other side of the hill. A typical room would be long but not particularly wide, with the ceiling being a curve. It reminds you of an underground train tunnel, it would not be difficult to imagine a tube train coming through the end wall and heading straight towards you. No cave house is the same and some even have more than one tier. In the local village there is one that has three distinct levels. Despite it being mostly underground, there seems to be enough windows to make my cave less gloomy than I would expect. Some people drill natural light shafts down, when they have a lot of dark rooms. The best time to enter a cave is after experiencing the full force of the summer sun. Suddenly you are in a cool shaded environment, unlike many of the village houses that suffer in the summer heat. In midwinter there is less need for heating, although it is a myth that Cave houses remain the same temperature both summer and winter, but they do hover around 14 to 18 degrees centigrade. If you look on the hill tops above cave systems you will see white chimney pots sticking up a bit like giant mushrooms. Somewhere beneath are open fires or log burning stoves, I have three in my cave system. I also like it in winter when it is howling a storm outside, but very little of its fury, encroaches on your cosy hobbit existence. Today's cave house is usually well appointed. The animal stalls are gone, replaced with shelving for books and CD's, and the kitchens have modern appliances and those near towns, have mains water and electricity. Those further out have septic tanks, personal water storage, and use solar panels or generators. Most of the caves have at least five or six rooms, mine has 19 and I have heard of others with double that number. One of my rooms has a rough pattern of lines in the roof. When you realise that these were made by someone's fingers, possibly a hundred years or more ago, it is impossible not to fit your hand into the impression they left, to compare.

When I drove up for the first time to my new home, after selling my first house in Spain. The place looked very different from my previous visit with the estate agent and a friend. The overgrown grass looked taller, the dilapidated outbuildings seemed more ready to collapse, and the cave rooms that had appeared cavernous and numerous had become smaller and more claustrophobic. The advertising blurb had said that all it needed was some minor repairs, and a good lick of paint. Well I suppose if the paint had been an inch thick and consisted of 90% concrete and applied to twenty two rooms, the estate agent may have been correct. The wall surfaces were little more than loose earth, which as it was basically a cave system would be expected, but did not lead to any feeling of security, knowing that above you was thirty or more feet of earth. In places crumbling lime wash or rough plaster patches had been applied with little effect. All of the rooms would have to be stripped back, re lined, including the curving ceilings, repaired and painted. Most of the doors were only five foot nothing tall, reflecting the average height of the previous bygone generations. Replacing some doors would not be the problem, cutting out an extra foot or so from the roof above to make it tall enough was going to be perilous, seeing as how tons of earth could flatten any amateur miner. I was later told, not to touch the ceilings but dig out the floor level instead, much safer. The floors for the most part were still bare earth or wafer thin cement; they would need levelling and tiling. Most of this work would have to be done by yours truly due to financial reasons, and at the then age of 59, with dodgy knees, I wasn't looking forward to it. Mind you I did have one consolation; I already had a lodger, Archie the bat. Unfortunately he didn't pay any rent or help with jobs, just kept buzzing me, whilst I laboured. In the end I think he got fed up with all the noise and dust and disappeared up the chimney in search of quieter premises. Actually he was not the only bat; I have some crumbling cave rooms at the far end of the property which are even today still unreformed due to their bad disrepair and likely collapse. I have re- named them the bat caves. If you go in quietly with a torch and shine it at the ceiling, numerous pairs of shiny eyes stare back at you. They were not the only residents; I had rats under an old chicken run, and mice that quite liked my rudimentary kitchen.

Slowly but not so surely the conversions have taken place, knocking down part of an attached wall, re-designing all the interior spaces within the courtyard wall, putting in extra windows and doors, taking off old roofs on the attached cottage and completely dismantling one whole level. It is fortunate that living out here in an old cave house, you can get away with bodging things much easier than if you lived in a street full of houses in England. The local council would not take kindly to me putting up a whole new set of buildings without planning permission, but the odd little change behind your boundaries tends to go un-noticed. I can create the most awful brickwork wall, then cover it entirely in Capa Fina (White cement) and nobody would be any the wiser. Mind you that is how a lot of them are build anyway. The most nervous job was deciding to pick my way through the earth to form a new corridor between two cave rooms. It was like going back a hundred years, covered in earth and wheel barrowing tons of rubble outside. Every moment you would check the ceiling for signs of cracks. Talking of cracks, most cave houses have them in the ceilings, even if the builder has covered them up. It is best not to mess with them too much unless they start to look really serious. Wire mesh frames can be concreted to the surface, which will hold things together a bit. But to be honest, if it decides to come down, then it will. In a local village they have had a lot of trouble; part of the hillside has collapsed and taken several cave houses with it. Two workmen died in one of them. This was after a particularly long spell of rain, which can soak down over a period of time.

Normally I don't think about what is above me and I have no problem with claustrophobia, but several friends are not so confident. They hover around the door area, rather than go too deep into the complex. My view is if it happens, it happens and I am not likely to know too much about it.

Being so far out, many of the cave houses have no electricity, water or mains sewerage. Some use solar panels or generators and for water, giant plastic containers that are normally perched high enough on the surrounding hills to generate a down flow. I was lucky or should I say canny in making sure that my cave was near enough to the road and dominated by some rather large electricity pylons. So I have both mains water and electricity, even if both go off, from time to time. At one point I had no water for six weeks whilst they dug up the countryside replacing ancient piping. Mind you it does have to travel about 10 km from the nearest deposito. The pipes are made of tough rubber and at points along the way are very close to the surface. This means that in the summer you get instant hot water that has a slightly odd taste. A friend, who lived in a cave house not far from me, was unfortunate in that an electric cable blew down across another, and sent 400 volts through the system of every home in that area. The result was that all of his electrical devises that were plugged in, started to internally melt. This included TV, fridge, stereo system, computer and all the wiring for the lights, amongst other things. I have a trip switch box that should in theory save me from such mishaps, but apparently for whatever reason his didn't work.

Sewage is another matter; we have to be self-contained. The caves usually have at least one Pozo Negro, connected to the system. Basically this is a large chamber dug into the ground. The original ones used bricks, but new regulations require that it is a giant plastic container with different compartments. I had to build an extra one a few years back and got a digger in to excavate a large hole. Into this went two enormous concrete tubes, end on and one on top of the other. Looking down into it was like looking down a tunnel to the centre of the earth. It was capped with a large slab of concrete with a tiny hole to let out the gases, otherwise one day it could all explode upwards like a rocket silo. My older one is looking decidedly dodgy, the top concrete crust is beginning to crumble, one day if I don't fix it, I or one of the dogs is going to descend rapidly into something quite nasty.

As I said the water has to travel a long way across country and many of the composite rubber pipes are well past their life expectancy, hence the local council are forever digging up bits of them all over the campo. You can tell when there is a problem because your water pressure drops right down and then stops completely, when they cut it off to do repairs. The thing is that they never tell you, just cut it, and then go off for the weekend in some cases. Last year I received three water bills all in the space of two months, each was for quadruple what they should have been, and I was only supposed to get two a year anyway. Apparently I was responsible for escaping water, even though it was not apparently happening on my land. Another friend of mine received a water bill for over three thousand Euro's, it seems that a local farmer had tapped into her supply and was busy watering all his olive groves. Another local Spanish farmer would turn up every month or so with a giant water lorry and fill up at night, by connecting up to our village system. Thousands of litres were being syphoned off and linked to someone's bill, perhaps it was mine.

Another problem is that the water around here has a disproportionate amount of calcium deposit in it. Pipes and kettles get furred up really quickly and even water purifying systems fail to cope. Every few months I have to get the plumber in to unclog my water heating system and normally remove the taps to get at the primary water filters. Most times you can fill a teaspoon with grey/white sludge that reduces the flow to a trickle. Just to think, how much of this stuff has passed through my system, in the years I have lived here. Recently I took the dog to the vets because she was leaking in the house. The vet took an x-ray and proceeded to show me that the poor thing was clogged up with what looked like snowflakes. This the vet pronounced was sand, but she meant calcium deposits. There was only a small space left for my dog to store pee. Now all my animals and I are on bottled water permanently. With six animals and me, we get through 5 litres a day, so the plastic bottles are mounting up. One thing that really makes me angry is the amount of plastic we use to wrap just about everything. As most of it is non-biodegradable we will eventually have a plastic coating around the earth. In the future archaeologists will be able to dig down through the strata and accurately pin point our century. So far I have made plant pots, water drip feed systems for the garden, and just about every food stuff in my kitchen has a converted plastic water bottle as its storage container. Now I am running out of ideas, but thankfully at least for Christmas the local council have come to my aid. They want everyone to bring their plastic bottles to them so that they can construct an ecological Christmas tree. They haven't said what they are going to do with them afterwards, but then again the local Spanish are known for not thinking that far ahead, just live for today.

I am really lucky that I am surrounded by great views. Most of it is taken up with Olive groves. It is a type of tree I hardly ever saw in my first fifty or so years of life, but have now become very familiar with. The ones round here are cultivated so that they have three trunks branching out from the root ball. This obviously produces a bigger crop. I love the rustle of the silvery green leaves when the wind blows.

CARS AND OTHER THINGS MOTORING

Maybe it is because I am now driving on the wrong side of the road, or that I navigate roundabouts by approaching on the right and then go anti clockwise around them, but I seem to be much more aware of my fellow drivers, than I was or should have been in England. It is not on the motorways and main roads that you notice much difference, you get those who think they are invincible, all over the world. It is on what we called the B roads and lanes that you get to witness the worst of driving attitudes.

First we have the tailgaters, who seem to proliferate around here, mind you they could be everywhere for all I know. Now if someone is rushing their wife to the hospital because she is about to deliver, or is a fireman heading for his fire engine, a loud blast on the horn and flashing of lights would have me moving out of the way quickly. I may be a bit grumpy, not knowing the reason, but I would sure move sharpish. But that is not the normal situation. You can see the whites of their eyes in the rear view mirror and the impatient strain on their faces. It is not because you are crawling along, just that they have an urgent need to gain five minutes on their journey, and possibly take twenty years off your life at the same time.

Then here in the campo we have the old guys, usually in battered old vans or new electric cars who think that 10 klm an hour is a sensible speed, it may be the best that some of these vehicles can do. At least I don't tailgate them; most times I pull over, admire the scenery and reflect on life for five minutes, if I can't overtake safely in the narrow lanes. You get the impression that more than a few of them never took a test.

Lately the police as well as making a hobby out of lying in wait at roundabouts to increase their fines tally, have been given lots of new regulations to check. The old days of having your seat belt on are simply not enough. Now you need a spare pair of glasses if you wear them, two yellow jackets, which must be worn if you break down, a complete set of light bulbs and two sets of warning triangles, at least the fire extinguisher and first aid kit are optional. There is an argument for having all these things, but the fines can be imposed for missing even one of them. All your vehicle documentation must be available and I don't mean copies, but the genuine articles, including passport or at least your residencia. Now should you be foolish enough to leave all this lot nicely in a folder, a car thief has all he needs to pose as you.

Just a few words of advice, to anyone considering driving in Spain. Using a cell phone whilst driving is not allowed, obviously, but so is having an earpiece attached to anything, likewise screen based navigation systems. Breath tests for alcohol are very stringent, 0.05% for experienced drivers and 0.01% for new and young drivers. In other words one glass of beer or wine would be enough. The other thing that even many Spanish don't realise is that the national speed limit of 120Klm an hour on motorways was reduced to 110, some time ago, but the signs have not been changed. Oh and watch out for Gorillas, unofficial men who wave you into parking places in exchange for a euro. The assumption being, if you don't pay, you may find a few marks on your car when you return. Pedestrian crossings are another thing to be careful at. Although the person crossing has right of way, many Spanish motorists don't agree with that ruling. Mind you a lot around here don't agree with signalling at all, let alone stopping for anyone else.

Unless you want a lot of trouble, never argue with the Guardia

Civil, they are a law unto themselves. There are cases of 500 euros on the spot fines for tourists who do not have the required paperwork, such as an International driving licence. No matter how aggrieved you feel, saying the wrong things could have your car impounded and you having to walk home. These are definitely not your courteous, helpful understanding Bobbies that you are used to.

Even if you have a Spanish driving licence, every few years you have to take some tests. Not your full driving test, it just consists of a medical and a reaction test. In my case I had to go to Granada and after registering at the police traffic centre they directed me across the road to what looked on the outside, to be a newsagents and general food store. However there was another door which led to a small room that had been partitioned off into four sections. The first compartment consisted of a desk with a very bored man in a white doctor's coat reading a newspaper. After the obligatory Spanish wait of a few minutes, whilst he finished reading the article that so absorbed him, he gave me a cursory once over with his stethoscope and pointed to the next cubicle, before going back to the sports page. There was no one in the next cubicle so I sat down and waited, after five minutes a white coated figure came in, it was the same man, obviously he reads a page between each operation. Instructing me to read various letters from a chart on the wall, first with and then without my glasses, he scribbled something on a slip of paper and pointed at the next cubicle. I never did find out what cubicle three was about because after another ten minutes my newspaper reading friend appeared muttering something about someone not being here. However he ticked the paper and pointed at the last cubicle. So I had obviously passed that bit, by just sitting patiently. May be it was a test to see if I was susceptible to road rage!

The last test was to see if my coordination had been shot to pieces by too much cheap Spanish wine. There was a computer console that looked like one of the early arcade machines and two storks sticking out of the desk. It was just what it appeared to be, a pre PlayStation arcade driving game. A basic road wove its way to an ever receding horizon. A ball rolled along and it was obvious that you had to control it with the two sticks, keeping it from leaving the road, and negotiating all the bends. The thing started up and I was instantly off the road, madly waggling the sticks I got a modicum of control, but it was only seconds before I was off the other side. This went on for ages, well at least ten minutes, by which time I was beginning to get mentally exhausted. I must have left the road at least fifty times, and was convinced that I had failed the test miserably. The problem was that one of the control sticks was over sensitive whilst the other was worn out and hardly effected the direction of the ball at all. I think that as ninety per cent of people are right handed, one stick had received far more punishment than the other. Judging by the way I and must assume everyone else had been yanking it about, it's surprising that it worked at all.

Going back to the first desk to receive my failed notice, I mentioned the worn out machine, but the guy just shrugged and handed me my paper. Apparently I had sailed through and was therefore allowed back on the roads of Spain for another five years or so. Before leaving I just had to mention that veering of the road fifty times was an unacceptable number of digital accidents. He grunted that the average was ninety, so I was apparently a comparatively safe driver. Being tailgated, almost forced off the road by a rather large lorry, and nearly being wiped out at a junction, all on the way back home, I tended to agree with him about the average Spanish motorist.

Old Cart on display in Castril

ATMOSPHERE AND HAUNTED

Driving back to my first stomping ground in Spain, after living in my new area for five years was very emotional. Not just meeting some of the locals, that had aged more than me, mind you I don't look in mirrors much. But the place, deep in the mountains, with whitewashed homes standing out from the olive green trees, looked better than I remembered it. The whole place reverberated beauty. I stopped at a spot where water cascaded down from the rocks and thought back to the hot summer days that I and my previous dogs, had withstood the shock of the ice cold water and bathed under it. I looked at the misty dawn as damp clouds rolled away all around me, leaving me and everything dripping wet. Two hours later and drying in the warmth, the whole mountain felt like it had been washed clean.

It is at times like these that you wonder why you moved. In my case it was just the need for a better house, and at least a garden for my animals. I almost purchased land there and in retrospect it may not have been a bad idea, but I love my cave house here, and the views are still good even if they can't quite compare.

Meeting even partial acquaintances again becomes like the re-uniting of long lost brethren. There is much back slapping and hugging, strange considering it was only the local grocery store owner, or one of the guys from the bar, who you had minimal contact with before. But this is Spain where that sort of expression of emotion is normal under those circumstances. If it was a town in England it would be a smile and a handshake.

My biggest mistake on the latest trip back, was to warmly hug and get into an animated conversation, with someone I had completely mistaken for someone else. I wondered why they had aged so much and kept giving me baffled looks. The trouble is that most locals like to please; they never tell you that they can't do something. Shops will always be able to get it by next week, or will phone you back. Unfortunately they rarely keep those promises. They just don't like to admit that the answer they should give is, 'no.' In this particular case, he obviously could not bring himself to say, "Who the f... are you?" Instead he kept nodding and smiling and accepted the drink I offered.

It was in the middle of the next day when I actually met the guy I thought the other person was, that the realisation dawned; I had been talking to a complete stranger, as if he was my best mate. That's the problem with allowing emotion to be effected by nostalgic atmosphere.

Why is it that places have atmosphere? Not only places, but streets, individual buildings, rooms or even particular corners of rooms, have their own presence. Up the hill from my old village, on the crest of a ridge there is a building that at one time in the past must have been majestic. It was built with turrets and arches, the garden had a lake and fountains. It reminded me of a cross between a Moroccan Palace and a English country house. Until a few years ago you could climb in through a window and wander the large interior rooms. It had classic murals on some of the walls, and floor tiles to die for. The kitchen had obviously been able to serve up banquets, and each room was pregnant with impressions. Unlike Britain it had not been trashed by yobs, or defaced with spray cans. In one room a rocking chair was still placed near the window. If it had started to move, I would have been out of there like a shot. Down in the large ground floor basement there was a wooden wagon and even more bizarre a German second world war jeep with Nazi insignia. Maybe I had stumbled on Hitler's bolt hole after the war. Winding my way up the stairs to the turreted battlements, you could see miles across the mountain range to tiny whitewashed villages.

I took a female friend to look around it, whilst she was on the battlements; I descend to the garden and took a photo of her, whilst her hair was streaming out in the wind. Every time I subsequently looked at that photo it made the hairs on my neck stand out. She looked like a ghost, a lost soul haunting the place, looking for her lost love. Almost made you want to start singing Heathcliff.

I forgot to mention why it feels so haunted, apart from its obviously interesting past. The local story was that at the end of the last century a wealthy landowner dis-inherited his son, because he had fallen in love with a beautiful long haired gypsy woman. The only thing he left him was this house. With no money the place slowly fell in to disrepair and the woman abandoned the son. He continued to live there on his own, more or less a recluse. Finally he tried to kill himself with a shotgun but only succeeded in disfiguring his face. No one knows what happened to him. Now this may be just a tale that has developed over the years in the local bar, but it sure adds to the impression you get, when walking around the place. Just across on another ridge is a square fortress, although it is obviously a lookout point and more of a folly, than genuine. But it bears similar characteristics to the house. There must be a link, but as yet I have not found any information.

Lately a friend of mine has shown interest in buying an old olive press building near my home. From the outside it looks like the building needs pulling down as the walls are cracked and the roof has partly fallen in. However saying that, it definitely has character and not for the first time I have thought it would make a great artist studio and gallery or craft complex. We managed to fight our way in past the overgrown brambles, to find a lost time inside. I have driven past numerous times and never guessed what was inside. Originally trucks would deposit the olives in assigned bays in the back walled courtyard which is the size of a small football field, you would never know it as there from the outside road view. But it is inside the main building, which is most impressive. Giant steel presses weighing God knows how many tons, have lain idle for at least 25 years, winding gear and massive hoppers, giant metal oil drums the size of two cars on end, and even a railway system with a turning circle in the floor on which heavy carts could be moved around inside. You had to be careful as there were several steel lined holes in the floor, some were full of water but one was empty and it was impossible to see the bottom. If you fell down there whilst on your own, no one would ever find you.

Should you perish down one of those holes, you would no doubt be given a procession, letting off loud exploding rockets every so often, up to the nice clean white cemetery on the edge of my village. Once there you would be placed in one of the concrete cubicles built into the numerous walls. Various marble attachments and engraved statements could adorn the sealed door and once upon a time you could also have your photograph stuck on the front. I found that the best bit of wandering round; you could see what the inhabitant actually once looked like. Think I will use the photo booth one of me, when my friend stuck his bare leg around the curtain. But it is not the new cemetery that has the atmosphere. Until recent complaints to the local council, the original cemetery on the other side of town was overgrown and abandoned. You could walk around and see open tombs, various human bones and bits of shroud. A small skull had been placed in a prominent position by someone and stared at you when you walked around the corner. Now that was one place I wouldn't have gone at night. As I said, it has now been cleared up, but it does tend to make you think that this show of honouring your ancestors, with such events as the day of the dead or marching bands and fireworks at your funeral, is more about the chance to have another day off work rather than genuinely caring about poor old grandma. Or am I just being a bit too much of a cynic?

I just can't help deviating slightly from Spain for a moment, because the story of the haunted house just reminded me of a stone house I stayed in, near York, many years ago. Being an artist and keen to paint new areas, someone had given me the keys to this place, so I could stay for a week or two and explore and paint the great landscape around there. Although there were other houses in the street, the moment I walked into the place, I felt very unnerved. I had taken my old collie dog, which only entered with great reluctance. There was nothing unusual about the place at first glance. No long gloomy corridors, it was a 300 year old stone house, but someone had open planned the ground floor. That night the dog slept on my bed for the first time in its life, and when I had a bath upstairs I left the door open so I could see down the corridor. I kept telling myself that I was stupid, after all some of the places that I had previously lived in had been far more remote. In the end a week was enough for me, and getting on the train home was genuine relief. The house had a cellar but there was nothing down there except stone seats down two sides and some strange little holes running the length of them. When I returned the key to the owner, I mentioned that I and the dog had felt very uneasy. It was only then that he told me its history. Apparently it had been a jail, the prisoners were chained up in the cellar, and hence the small holes in the wall. It was not a permanent jail for them, most spent one night before being led down into town and hanged. If you had enough money you could bribe the jailer to cut your throat instead of facing the hangman, apparently that was preferable. I asked him if he ever stayed there, "You must be joking," was his reply.

FILM CAREER

I was sipping a nice cool beer in the bar I sometimes frequented in Baza. Each Friday evening I had somehow got myself the job of, singing and playing guitar to a handful of people who generally ignored me until they had had a few beers and then they would join in, mostly out of tune.

One particular night I noticed an advert pinned to the wall, requesting anyone who fancied being an extra in a film to contact the local council office. Anything for a laugh I filled the accompanying form in and where it asked if the person had any experience acting, I mentioned that I had appeared in two plays. What I did not say was that one was a non-speaking part, in which I just appeared at a window for five seconds and the other only ran for two days. I wrote out the application in English and Spanish, just to show willing and took it to the offices the next day. The most interesting information was the part that said that the extras would be paid and fed. As it turned out they got free T-shirts and stale sandwiches. However that was not to befall me, I was destined for bigger things, move over Marlon Brando.

There were hints that it would be a biblical epic, funded by the regional Government and using local landmarks. So the local lake would become the Sea of Galilee, the surrounding barren hills, where Jesus wanders in the wilderness, and unreformed caves to become dwelling places. When filming started they had to remove the plastic boats from the lake side, as it would not have looked historically correct. As it was the mocked up fishing boat they used for the scene where Jesus and the disciples get away from the crowds, started to partially sink, he didn't manage to walk on water this time, pity they didn't keep that bit in the film.

Sitting in the ante-room with several other men my age and all sporting beards, I began to wonder what part I was up for, it was not as an extra, they had been picked on mass. One guy came out and told us we would have to read a bit of script. When it came to my turn I hid my glasses, so that I would look more in keeping with biblical times. Entering the large room I could just make out, with my now impaired vision, three people sitting at a desk at the far end. Apparently I shook the hand of the least important but most impressive looking one first; he turned out to be the accountant. The Director was a small man who looked more like an office clerk.

Luckily my short focus is ok, so when they handed me a script and told me to read the part of an apostle in English, I did not make a fool of myself. Mastering my best Sir Laurence Olivier impression I launched into it, but after thirty seconds they stopped me. Oh! I thought, well that did not go down too well. But the pause was brief, as they produced a towel from somewhere and asked me to drape it over my head. Now I may not be very good looking, but I thought it was a bit much to give me the paper bag on head treatment. Apparently they just wanted to see if I looked native enough and not a pale Brit in disguise.

After I had finished they made approving nodding actions and told me to wait for a decision. Three other men, two boys who did not have beards, and a really old guy went in after me; they all looked more suitable to be wearing a towel on their heads than me. However it turned out that I got the part of John the Apostle as an old man, looking back on his life, the cheek of it, the old man bit I mean. The two boys got bit parts, as did two of the other men, but I had twenty pages of script to learn and eventually ended up appearing in fourteen scenes. The best part was they gave me over one thousand euro for my efforts and I didn't even have an acting card.

I have to admit that the film was crap. If you can find a CD of it at a second hand market, it is called El Dicipulo or The Disciple, in English. I did go and watch it in a cinema on the big screen, it was weird seeing myself up there, especially as they had dubbed my voice after all that, and I sounded like a fifty cigarette a day addict. At the end, I turned around when the lights went up to see if anyone recognised me, but was totally ignored, but that was not surprising, seeing as how they had given me a dark tan and blacked out half my teeth for the part.

When the morning came for filming my bits, I arrived at makeup to be kitted out in robes and powdered wig. I don't know if they thought I was a real actor, but at one point I had someone doing my hair, whilst another did my makeup. Meanwhile the dresser was standing patiently at the side ready to transform me. Then there was the personal assistant who never seemed to leave my side. He was an earnest young man, who kept asking me if I needed a drink, a cigarette, or to run over my lines with me. A taxi then took us across town to the location site. It was funny looking out at the town I walked around normally when shopping, but here I was dressed like an apostle with a bright red face. Apparently they have to overdo the colour for the lighting effects. My mind was blank whilst sitting waiting for the director to shout shoot, or something like that; I could not remember a single line until the moment my mouth opened. Around me up to thirty people, cameramen, lighting technicians, soundmen, assistants and even fire and safety officers, who had to light the flaming torches in brackets on the wall. At first I was awestruck by it all, but after a while you realise it is five minutes filming and then an hour whilst everyone rushes around sorting things, I just sat there. The worst moment was when I was told I had to get emotional in the next scene and allow a tear drop to roll down my face. It was suggested that I spent the hour waiting, by thinking of sad events in my life, although the tear would be fake water. By the time they came to shoot I was an emotional wreck, thinking back about my parents and partner that had all sadly passed away.

I won't go on about my one chance at stardom, but there were a couple of side events worth mentioning. Not many people can say that they had a fried breakfast with Jesus, and he gave me his bacon. We also had no toilets on the set, when it was being filmed in an old Moorish bath house. We had to walk over to a local bar. Some of the locals knew what was going on, but others walking in were confronted with the site of Jesus and a couple of apostles and their security guard, lining up for the only toilet cubicle.

STEALING TILES DOESN'T PAY

I know that I shouldn't have been stealing the rustic roof tiles of the old abandoned school house, but after all it was almost on my land, well at least up to its front door anyway. The place was falling down and even the council didn't care. Seemed a shame to just let them drop and smash when the roof caved in, as it surely would very soon. Anyway there I was up the top of my folding ladder, when it decided to do what came naturally to it, and folded. Now bearing in mind that it was getting dusk, I was in the campo (countryside) of rural Spain, with no houses or people around and very rough terrain full of prickly, spiky things. My saviour was a friend (Well he is now) who was on his first full week as a permanent resident in the country, and I was trying to show him how handy we all were out here in the wilds. He tried to lift 17 stone of body with a leg that seemed to want to go in a different direction, but soon gave up. It was fairly evident that I wasn't going to walk or even hop home down a precarious slope and that my only course of action was to crawl on all fours in the other direction, across a semi ploughed field to a track where he could drive his car and pick me up. By this time it was getting dark, but there was still enough light for a local farmer to mistake me for a large wild pig and take a pot shot, as they are prone to do during the hunting season. Apart from watching the headlights of my friends car as he got lost and drove into a quarry, nothing much else happened apart from finding myself parked on a trolley in an abandoned plaster room at the local hospital for two hours, whilst my leg slowly increased to treble its normal size. They kept me in for three days, told me I needed screws in my leg but that they could not operate till the swelling and giant pressure blisters had gone down. The choice was to spend the next three weeks waiting in a hospital bed or go home. I went home, have you tasted hospital food?

Ignoring the fact that I had spent three weeks in a cave house with a wobbly leg, then used my crutches to hop the entire length of the hospital, up three flights of stairs and attempted to sign into the wrong ward, they still insisted on placing me in a wheelchair at the reception desk, and then pushing me 20 yards to my appointed bed. From that moment on I began to find the hospital systems more and more hilarious and that is what I am going to regale you with over the course of this chapter, so bad luck.

I don't mean to be nasty about Spanish hospitals; after all I have had a hernia operation, knee replacement and now a broken leg. In fact I should be very grateful because, after all, I don't pay into their Social Security System. (Word of warning, don't go abroad without your E111 card.) But laying there in a hospital bed with nothing to do but think and observe, it starts to be very funny when you see how things are done, so here is the rant of a grumpy old man in Spain.

In hospitals I believe they have a plan to de-humanise you; make you feel insignificant, even the simplest request seems as if you have asked for the moon. Unlike the old days of rows of beds, the hospital I was in had small rooms with only two beds per room, which at least was an improvement; however it came with its own set of problems. They have a policy here that it does not matter how many relations you have in the room, as long as there is room for some of them to sit on the other patient's bed. I was told the record was held by a gypsy family that had 35 relatives turn up, and the guy wasn't even dying. The Spanish can all talk at once and still seem to have a conversation; mind you it usually sounds more like an argument. The fact that there is someone in the next bed hoping for a little peace and quiet is of no consequence. Now I am as tolerant as the next person, but when the first visitor turns up in the morning, and once gone is replaced by another, then another, until it is suddenly 11pm. My two visitors who came seems a little outnumbered (not to say unfair). So when the person in the next bed has talked themselves hoarse and collapsed into loud snoring, you lay back and let out a deep sigh. Then the pain starts, where was it all day when it might have taken my mind of other things? It may have made me irritable enough to attack the other patient's visitors with my full bedpan, which incidentally I had to fill and asked to be emptied on several occasions, whilst being observed by several pairs of eyes.

 As the pain increases you try to ignore it and start fidgeting in the hope of finding a strange angle of limbs that eases the situation, but of course it doesn't. Fearing using the panic button and asking for some painkillers ,sleeping pills or even a mallet to the head, you leave it as long as you can bare it. Inevitably you press the red button and way down the corridor you hear a faint bleep that repeats every few seconds. In the silence, you even find yourself holding your breath. Nothing! No response, have they all gone home, are you and your snoring friend all alone in an empty hospital? Ten minutes later after a respectful wait, you dare to try again. Suddenly the intercom crackles and a voice loud enough to wake my neighbour who grunts in disgust at being disturbed, shouts "Que Quieres?" (What do you want?) I felt like saying "Burger and large French Fries, what the F... do you think I want? Help, give me morphine, knock out pills, even a saw to cut this damn leg off," Instead I feebly asked for a pain killer. Still no one comes for ages, then shuffling feet getting closer until with a disgruntled sigh, a nurse who has also been just woken from her cat nap in the duty room, utters a stream of Spanish that my neighbour obviously agrees with but which I understand little. However at a guess it probably translated as something like. "Why are you such a wimp? You had pain killers three hours ago and that is all you should have till the morning, but I suppose I can make an exception for you weak foreigners, now stop assuming the foetal position and take this" Then with a parting comment that probably meant " Don't trouble me again," she was gone. Oh and the painkiller, it was one measly Paracetamol.

Sometimes they come un-called for, throw on the main light, check something or other, ask a question in a loud voice, click off the light and don't bother to shut the door, leaving you sitting bolt upright and wide awake at 3am. There was one nurse and to be fair she was one of the few kind ones, who would come and check on you, and rather than put the main light on to disturb the other patient, she had a torchlight strapped to her forehead. The first thing you would be aware of was an intense beam of light, like something out of Star Wars or The Great Escape, flashing round the room as she examined the drip or searched for the sleeping pill in her pocket, until it finally settles on your face and blinded you so that you couldn't see that she was holding it out to you. "No thanks, actually I was asleep till you decided to blind me."

I think at some time or another we have all experienced the interminable endless hours of night. If you are lucky you don't have someone snoring incessantly in the next bed. The worst are those that appear to be dead, then explode in a loud earth shattering snort followed by various gurgles, sinus squeaks then silence again. You end up counting the seconds between each eruption, nothing better if you suffer from high blood pressure. Finally as it is just starting to get light outside you drift into blissful sleep, 'Aghh' the dreaded mobile phone with the ever repeated few bars of the Entry of the Toreadors drags you back through the befuddled layers of sleep. The blasted guy in the next bed who was annoyed at me for calling for a nurse, is shouting down his mobile something about having a disturbed night and will the family be in this morning to see him, I look at my watch, it's seven in the bloody morning.

Then you drift off again only to be woken an hour later by the first of the days routines. Discounting the Entry of the Toreadors you get the entry of the clean sheets lady. Her sole job is to place new bed linen on a chair by the bed, for others much later in the morning to change. She could do it quietly but that is not the Spanish way.

"Hola Buenos Dias" at the top of her voice.

"Sod off, just because you are up and alive, doesn't mean I want to be."

This little scenario is then repeated at regular intervals over the next hour or so by the nurse that takes your temperature, another nurse to take your blood pressure, the room cleaning lady who is the only one who insists on wearing a mask, just in case I am contagious, or maybe she is? Oh boy! Then comes breakfast which normally consisted of a crusty roll left over from yesterday, together with an over ripe tomato and a blunt knife so you end up splatting it all over the tray. A little pot of olive oil that you can't peel the lid off without the same result, and a cup of warm sickly milky liquid that is meant to be coffee . As a result you are left hunting for the bar of chocolate that you hid from yesterday, whilst your bed has a distinctly "After the picnic" look about it.

Another little trick to dehumanise you is to give you an undersized smock to wear. This piece of material is open sided and open backed, generally with at least some of the string ties missing. The reason I am told, is so that the doctor on his rounds can gain easy access. Personally I found that the last thing the doctor wanted to do on his rounds was actually examine you. This garment is embarrassing enough anyway, almost impossible to cover all your private parts, on a hop to the loo with twenty people in the room and your arse sticking out. Being six foot tall and 17 stone, the biggest one they had was a medium; it wasn't far short of a mini skirt length. Now I don't like to boast, but it also caused me embarrassing problems at the front as well as the back. To cap it all they came in nice shades of pink or yellow with polka dots all over them, I ask you! May be they have an arse of the week competition and need to regularly check by way of the demeaning bed bath routines, which happened whether or not you could do it yourself.

Just to show how subservient you become, one day the nurse asked me what I was writing about. I should have said some notes about the standard of hospital service (Which I was) but being a chicken I just said, "oh just a letter".

Right, now I am only just getting started. Bed pans, well to be more precise a plastic bottle, not big enough to hold two pees worth, so you end up desperately trying to hold back a portion for fear of overflow. Having spent my life training myself not to pee in bed, it comes very hard to lay there and purposely do it. You have to lay there and let it go, let's hope it doesn't become a habit. It is not as if I had consumed large amounts of water (or illicit beer cans, stored in my bottom locker, under my spare pants.) It's all those endless packs of liquid gloop they keep hooking you up to, if I'm so full of fluid that I have to keep regularly calling the nurse for my bed pan to be emptied, it's their fault, not mine.

Right! next complaint, the bloody open door. They give you a nice little room for two, then insist that the door remains open at all times, so that the hordes of visitors passing down the corridor looking for their friends or relatives just have to peer in. As there is hardly a moment in the day when the corridors are not thronged, then you are almost constantly under observation. I found that by leaning out to a point of overbalancing out of bed, and using my crutch I could push our door shut, then lay back with a sigh only for it to be thrust open by someone looking for a relative. "Perdone esta es 312?" "No it ruddy isn't can't you read the number on the door" but by then they had gone. At a rough estimate I doubt it was much under thirty times a day on average that unwelcome guests thrust the door open, after I had closed it. Then there are those Spanish who love animated arguments right outside your door, they go on for ages, but don't do it outside the door of their ailing relative, because they are generally talking about them, and who gets what in the will.

I was being wheeled in my bed round most of the hospital, on my way to have a second set of x-rays to see how the screws had taken. All was well until the return journey, with a different person pushing. First we demolished a waste paper bin, and then got stuck in the lift, when the doors got wedged on the bed. This needed the assistance of a group of strangers who were passing by, to un-wedge it. Then we finally emerged on the wrong floor and got lost. The person pushing had to phone to find out where my room was; anyway it broke the boredom of the day. I know I am complaining but what else had I got to do, but lay there for hours on end constructing conspiracy theories, and getting annoyed or amused by events.

Now I know that this is grossly unfair on all my friends who cared enough to come and visit me in hospital, and I was glad to see them, especially if they came bearing goodies. But there is a big difference between chatting to your friends over a beer or cup of tea, than sitting facing them from a hospital bed, whilst they take it in turns to share the only visitor's chair. Natural conversation is almost impossible, and you can see that after fifteen minutes when they have asked you how you are feeling and what the food is like and in a whisper what is wrong with the man in the next bed, (is he dying because it looks like his whole family are crammed into the other half of the room?) they are thinking, how long before it's considered ok to leave. It is amazing how "Can't leave the dog too long" is the stock excuse. I know what you are thinking, "This guy is such a moaner, no wonder they want to get away." But honestly I try to put on a cheery face and keep all these dark thoughts to myself. Mind you I did tend to share my bed pan experiences with most visitors, maybe that's why they left early.

I'm not running out of hospital complaints yet, here are just two short ones. The Hospital soup that was only good for washing plates. All the meals without salt, yes I know I have got slightly high blood pressure, what do you expect, I'm in here, in pain and with one measly Paracetamol.

Paperwork, paperwork, they just love it. If they can find a more difficult way of doing something, then they will. Turning up for check-ups, you are confronted by hordes of people and one little door, which if you are lucky will open once in a blue moon for someone in a white coat to dart out, and try and make it to the canteen. However it is like someone firing a starting pistol, everyone lunges forward with their little piece of paper and tries to ram it in the white coats hand, or for that matter anywhere else it can be wedged. The fact that it says on your little scrap of paper, that your appointment is 9.30, means absolutely nothing. It is already nearly eleven and being British, you still haven't managed to hand your paper over; it is surprising how quickly the walking wounded can move when they want to. Why can't they just have a slot in the door, for people to post their appointments as they arrive, or better someone at a desk enrolling everyone? After finally seeing the medic on duty it was gone 12, but the day was only starting. I was sent for yet another x-ray, as if they didn't already have enough to clip together and make a short movie out of them. My word! There was someone at a desk at the x-ray department. Standing before her I presented my new slip of paper from the medic down the corridor.

"No, you have to get it stamped."

"But the doctor just gave it to me."

"It's not stamped."

"It's me, look I have a broken leg, I have my passport, and I don't want to spend my life in this hospital. Look at some of the people sitting waiting; they have been here so long, that they have lost the will to live." (Didn't really say that, but wish I had thought of it at the time.)

"It needs to be stamped."

"Who the hell is going to impersonate me?" (OK didn't say that either) can't you phone through and ask them, they have just sent me here? (Did say that)

"No it needs to be stamped."

Bear in mind, the queue behind me stretched out of the door, and I would have to go back to charging at the white coat all over again, like I had been doing for the last two hours. I was beginning to feel like some of the cobweb covered people sitting on plastic chairs in every conceivable alcove. I take my seat and peer at the single door, waiting for the handle to start turning. By this time I'm on first name terms with those around me. I know that the lady on my left has six children, and a husband with a bad back. The man on the other side says that he was trapped under his tractor when it tipped over on a steep slope. I said he was very lucky to be alive. He said that he had only got a broken arm, but the tractor would need a bit of fixing. I didn't even get the satisfaction of thrusting my bit of signed paper under the X-ray receptionist's nose, when I finally got back, she had gone for lunch.

I've been poking fun at the hospital system, but really the joke is on me. They pick up the pieces of our follies, and do what they can. Their procedures may often be chaotic but it is still a lot better than people have in many areas of the world, and I should be grateful.

For me the post operation shenanigans have been more amusing to write about because I have only myself to laugh at. After a blissful week recovering at the house of my Spanish friends Sergio and Maria, where my every whim (well almost) was catered for, I was deposited at my cave house with the prospect of coping on one leg on my own. The medico did come out to see me once, but seemed more interested in looking at my paintings than my leg. She did tell me to get rid of all my rugs in case I tripped. Didn't dare tell her that I had already done that and ended up on my backside with the broken leg held high out of harm's way during the fall, she never returned.

Now bearing in mind I could not put my broken leg on the floor even to balance and my crutches were little better than walking stick size, it became a battle of wills to get anything done. Hanging out the washing was always a good one. Assuming you have managed to somehow drag the basket outside by attaching some rope or such to your belt, washing lines are usually above head height so to bend down pull out some heavy wet jeans lift them up and peg them whilst on one leg and with only one hand because the other is holding a crutch to keep you from toppling, is a matter of some skill. One peg is not enough so you let go of your crutch and make a grab for the line which then begins to sway. Finally you reach equilibrium and stand there holding the line wondering how you can reach your stick. Now you have done one item of clothing, only another dozen to go. Sheets get hurled over the line, sod stretching them out, what's a few creases anyway. I also have to mention that my one good leg has a knee that isn't mine. It is a ball and plate prosthesis, put in a few years back and quite keen on sending me sideways at any moment.

Now what about cooking, let's take frying a couple of eggs for breakfast, nothing could be simpler, Ha! Only those flash cooks on the TV can crack an egg into a saucepan with one hand whilst not breaking them. I had to lean against the gas cooker to use both hands, not really advisable when wearing nylon track suit bottoms, because they are the only ones that will fit over my giant foot plaster. And what about carrying a nice mug of tea, to your favourite chair? The answer is you don't unless you want a wet floor, and quarter inch of tea left in the mug when you arrive. You take a flask in a bag around your head, but it's not the same somehow. (Try the bag method with a bunch of logs for the fire.)

OK so I have over egged the descriptions a bit, but it makes for funnier reading, and is more or less the truth. My solution was to cook, eat and drink in one place, keep it simple, spaghetti with everything and an orange for pudding. I suppose you could position a chair at every critical action station, but that is far too organised for me, and how do I move the chairs there in the first place. For those of you with nice neighbours a few yards away or a loving partner or family I need to explain why I end up with all these problems. Firstly I live in a cave house, literally miles from anywhere; you can't even see the lights from another dwelling at night. Yes I have friends who pop in to make sure I am still alive, but I am an independent old sod and find it hard to keep asking people for help when I think I can manage. However it is one of the few times in my life when I wished I had a partner to wait on me hand and foot, but that is more than I deserve.

HOUSES

I was driving home from the airport near Granada and noticed rows of the most appallingly designed new houses. Firstly they were adjacent to the motorway; secondly the view in any other direction was either non-existent because you would be looking into your neighbour's bedroom, or across to an industrial and trading estate. Added to this they were designed to look like little castles with buttresses and tiny towers, all they needed was a flag pole. Do they think we are all knights in armour or a Princess waving from the turret? Now I am well aware that many people have little choice about where they live, for financial reasons. Someone will always be thankful for a tenth floor flat in a rundown housing estate. I don't mean to be flippant about that. But these places were obviously not cheap, so who in their right mind would buy one. This is such a lovely diverse country with astounding views, wonderful sunsets, so why would you opt for seeing the arse end of a supermarket block? Even if your argument was that you needed easy access to the motorway, and the town centre, what is wrong with the small villages just a mile or so away? If the half-finished buildings you see everywhere are anything to go by, then these monstrosities are made of cement blocks, they will have no real insulation or double glazing, and you will no doubt be able to hear your neighbour snoring.

I have seen other housing down on the coast that is not much better, just because they are painted blisteringly white with rampant cement horses on the communal gateposts, or Moroccan motifs above the windows, doesn't make them classy, desirable or anything other than rows of boxes. The gated communities that seem popular with retired British are a bit better. At least most of them have a lawn area and communal swimming pool and boast most modern conveniences; some even have their own golf course. If you like that kind of security and bland existence where you hardly ever meet or get involved with local Spanish, preferring to play cards, indoor bowls or watch British TV, then I am not going to criticise your choice of lifestyle, it is just not for me. I can also see that many people would think my choice of a cave house miles from anything, would be their idea of hell.

Spain has rapidly converted its southern and eastern borders from pretty little fishing villages into major and not so major tourist hotspots. The amount of building has been phenomenal in the last twenty years. Unfortunately the boom has somewhat subsided, leaving numerous sites half completed. Many blame the present crisis and corruption problems, on what was called the "Marvellous Decade" when Spain concentrated its economy on the housing bubble. Recent figures suggest that house prices have now dropped as much as 44%, and some 1.5 million workers have lost their jobs in the construction sector.

Towns like Benidorm, Alicante and Fuengirola have become synonymous with cheap package flight holidays. The beaches in August are packed, and in winter almost empty. Those on a small pension can spend three winter months holed up in a hotel on the coast of Spain, and live cheaper than they could back home in their own house. The skyline of Benidorm is like a miniature version of New York from a distance. I once spent a miserable week high up in one of those holiday apartments. On both sides was the constant thumping of drum and bass music from two adjacent discotheques, the kitchenette had its own resident family of cockroaches, and I was on the eighteenth floor.

SAD STATE OF AFFAIRS IN SPAIN

I was sitting outside on a bench when the first street dog wandered up, in hope of something to eat. He was half starved and covered in tics, but still wagging its tail and hopeful. It only took a pair of pleading eyes and there I was ripping open the bag of dried cat food pellets that I had just brought along with a little shopping. Sprinkling a handful on the ground I watched him hoover them up in seconds, before turning on the soulful expression again. Having had another handful he settled down under my legs whilst we both waited for the world to turn some more. Fifteen minutes later and the word had got around that there was a sure touch with a bag of food. I had five dogs all sitting patiently in a semi-circle and eying my shopping bag. These strays get kicked and shouted at by the locals but they are still better behaved than my ones at home. Some of them have serious health problems ranging from mange to leismania (very common out here, caused by the bite of a sandfly.) It is to their shame that the government and local councils do very little to sort this problem out. I know one local sanctuary that although started by three Spanish men, only stays open and funded, because us foreigners get involved. Apart from a few kind souls, the local Spanish take no interest. Maybe it is asking too much of a country that likes killing Bulls for sport, and trapping singing birds in tiny cages, leaving them hanging from white hot walls, in the full glare of the sun. Most rural dog owners do not bother to have their animals sterilized but let them breed freely; the pups are often drowned at birth or just abandoned. I should like to think that I am being over dramatic, but unfortunately I am not. Thankfully some more enlightened parts of Spain such as Cataluña are waking up to the situation and there is a sea change, especially amongst the younger generations. Some people are kind to their pets in this part of the country, especially those better educated. I once remonstrated with an old farmer who had a dog chained up permanently. I asked him why he was so cruel; he just did not see my point of view, saying that "Dogs had no souls." This completely floored me, and the only thing I could think to say was that in English, God spelt backwards is Dog, and if God is a dog, then the local Spanish are in real trouble in the afterlife.

I just want to add that that only last week, I stopped to give a stray on the side of the road some food. As I bent down I heard a squeak from the bushes. There on a bit of old cardboard were six seriously undernourished puppies, only a week or so old. Having told my friends at the animal shelter, Matilda a kind and caring friend came with me and took them all home including the mother. She then spent several sleepless nights nursing them all back to some form of health. She already has at least half a dozen dogs; I don't know how she copes. She is not the only kind person taking in strays, a lot of the British do. They may say when they first arrive that they are not going to get lumbered, but it doesn't take long before one or two find a home with them. Some cannot stop and end up with numerous pets that keep them seriously busy, and out of pocket. The dog shelter has about thirty five dogs in it at the moment , all looking for homes, doesn't matter what country you live in if you are interested in adopting one, there is Info at end of the book. This local shelter has a tiny outside run for the animals; it is on an Industrial estate, in a large block unit, with no heating in winter. The dogs are kept in metal cages with sawdust on the floor. Once a day volunteers go in and clean their cages, give them food and a short walk up on scrap land. This means that for 22 hours of their day they are shut in on their own, with little or no stimulation or human contact. Let me stress that

the volunteers are all dog lovers and none of them are happy with the situation, but what little money is raised goes on the dogs care, and it is better than those dogs being on the street, starving. Depending on how long this book has been out in print, there should still be a Video on YouTube showing the state of affairs, here is the link
https://www.youtube.com/watch?v=UWomIC75_jI&feature=youtu.be

   There should be a National programme for sterilisation, within a few short years the situation of thousands of dogs literally starving to death would be sorted. Dog sanctuaries get little or no help from the local councils or Government. It is disgraceful, I think it was Ghandi who said that you can tell the degree to which a country is civilised, by the way they treat their animals.

Lake Negratin

WORK ETHIC AND THE ROAD TO WHERE?

Despite taking every chance they can get to have a fiesta, one thing I can say is that the Spanish in Andalucía have a work ethic grounded in hard graft. It may be a throw over from the days when everyone in this part of the world had to toil long hours on the land to survive, but they sure put in the hours. Even the office staff who are dedicated to preserving their jobs by making it impossible for anyone else to understand ,are very creative in inventing extra convoluted ways to do things. But I am getting off the point. Even if at the bottom of it all is the desire to make money, in general they certainly deserve it. Unlike several British builders I have known, the Spanish labourer will work his allotted eight hours and get far more done. They do have a pride in their abilities, and I am often amazed at how fast they work, yet still retain a degree of quality craftsmanship. The bar owners put in excessive hours each day and take little in the way of annual holidays. As I have said before, they know how to enjoy themselves when a fiesta day comes around, except for those behind the bar who are still working.

They may work hard but it's not always obvious, road repair around here seems completely random. But firstly, why would I regularly travel a road that's main aim is to bust your suspension. I still visit the thermal pool restaurant that I saw the first time I arrived in this area. The best time to go is in the middle of winter, when it is snowing, normally it will still open and you may be the only one there. Once in the water, with steam rising around your ears and snowflakes drifting down, it is a sublime experience. Mind you getting out is not quite so pleasant as the facilities are quite basic. There are two concrete cubicles, like ice boxes. It is better to just rub furiously and jump around, till you have some clothes on. In the summer it is very popular and gets a bit crowded, but then you can find a spot down by the lakeside and sunbath. They have now built a pontoon for tourists to jump in the lake from, but sadly it now seems to be a place for teenagers to park their cars and have loud rap music thumping out, whilst they splash about.

The funny thing is they have now built a brand new sports centre just further up the lakeside. It has two thermal swimming pools, one of which is inside and has all the normal things like sauna and solariums. I went in to enquire and during the hour I was looking around they didn't have a single customer. This is not so surprising, as the condition of the road leading to this area is now appalling. There are great chunks missing out of the tarmac caused by erosion, every time the nearby canal overflows it floods the road. Often it is covered in mud and there is a big sign saying that the road is only for building and access for council vehicles. Seeing as this road leads to two thermal centres, an expensive hotel, the lake where they hope to attract tourists, and as a short cut to nearby villages and the local mountain, with brilliant tourist views in all directions. You would think they would repair that first, before building everything else. But that is something I have observed a lot out here, there is not much logic to a lot of what goes on. Apparently what I have been told is that two local councils are quarrelling over whose responsibility this part of the road is, and both are waiting for each other to do something about it. Every year or so someone empties into the holes, the remainder of the tarmac used on other projects. For a week or so the road becomes passable, but when the first rains come and the canal floods, they are washed out again. For me it is the quickest way to the local big town and because the road also slopes sideways most of the holes are on two thirds of its width. The inevitable happens and everyone drives on one side, which causes a few heart palpitations when coming round the bends, to be met by a vehicle coming straight towards you. The last time it rained really heavily, a large lake appeared in one of the dips. My Spanish friend got halfway through it, and then stalled with water coming in over his door sills, inside the car were his wife and an older relative, he had to abandon them with their legs in the air, whilst he waded out to get help. After they finally got home and their car was towed away for drying out, he ended up in bed for several days with a very bad cold.

The local councils don't have a lot of money, even the road to the council offices in my local village was in a state of semi repair for months, closed off due to the fact that the outgoing Mayor had run out of money, and the new one was left with nothing but debts. Some of the local lanes have been tarmacked, but in order to save money they seem to have only been made wide enough for one and a half cars. The way that some locals drive, which is basically down the middle and at rather high speeds, has caused more than one accident. I am often literally forced off the road and into the dust of the orchards, by drivers who have no intention of moving over or slowing down. The large animal trucks visiting the chicken farms are the worst, and the dust carts are not much better, you can end up ankle deep in mud between olive trees. Sometimes you wonder why a particular piece of road has been reformed, whilst other more important ones have been left in a poor state. That is till you realise who owns the land that it leads too. In my previous village the only tarmac road outside the village, led to the mayor's, daughter's house. The majority of tracks across the Campo are just dirt, but they are often used more than some of the more main roads. That is not hard to understand, because in the past the farmers would just drive the shortest or most suitable route between places. These became suitable tracks for everyone to use. If you scan down on Google earth you will see the countryside in Spain, full of criss-crossing tracks. It may not rain much here, so your car tends to stay quite rust free, but your suspension sure takes a pounding, especially on these dirt tracks. If it does rain then they develop nasty ridges and gullies running down and across, depending on which way the rivers of water sought an escape. Then they are really difficult in anything short of a 4x4. Some of the bridges are little more than concrete slabs over the streams and often there is a ford down into the water that the larger vehicles use to cross. The streams can be deceptive and run faster than you think, I have seen foolhardy motorists get halfway and realise the error of their ways. Coming home from a Halloween party at about two in the morning ,I had the option of two routes, one way was the main road, but would go in a big loop and take about 35 minutes, or the other way was across country, using the dirt tracks and would literally only take 10 minutes. It was quite dry and the sky was clear and full of crisp stars, what could possibly go wrong. I had been from the other direction once, but that had been during the day, still, how hard could it be? The other reason was that I had got rather more alcohol in my system than was permitted. It was Halloween and the police would no doubt be all geared up with their little throwaway plastic mouth pieces. The dirt track would be thankfully free of police cars, and finished right near my home. Unfortunately I didn't see the turnoff I should have taken, and preceded along a track that looked remarkably similar, one Olive grove looks much like another in the dark. After a while a shallow ditch appeared across the road, but I crossed it without much trouble, then another which took a bit of revving to get out of. The third one looked a trifle deeper, so I stopped and got out to take a look. The depression was only a foot or so deep but the two edges had quite an angle to them, but I had driven over worse before, so I went for it. Going in I managed to scrape my exhaust pipe, but that was nothing, because I could not get out the other side. The wheels were deep in powdery earth and the rim too much of a sudden ledge. I was stuck, it was gone two o'clock in the morning, it was the wrong track, so God knows where I was, and I was dressed up as Freddie Kruger with a false pointed nose and a shirt I had carefully painted slashed ribs on. At least I had taken the false hand with razor sharp claws off. Sometimes there are moments in your life when you just stand there and sigh very loudly, with your shoulders slumped and your arms hanging slackly. I had two choices, walk home or gun the engine and sod the exhaust pipe. Somehow I turned the car around and charged at the original banking. For a second I did not think I was going to make it, but somehow the car clawed its way out and I was off like a mad thing. The two other ditches, I had crossed earlier, were taken at an alarming rate, bouncing around like a lunatic. If someone had seen me dressed up as I was, they would have run screaming. Needless to say I found the right turning and arrived home safely. The ten minute trip had taken an hour and fifteen minutes.

The Mayor of Baza who seems to be the person who decides just how much the satellite towns will receive, has been recently criticised for keeping most of the money to spend on tarting up his own town for personal glorification. Hence Baza has ornate roundabouts with commissioned sculptures, denoting points of local historic or cultural interest, grassed walkways, cycle paths and a brand new three floor library that always seems empty when I go in it. Meanwhile the outlying villages have trouble funding basic repairs to water supply and roads.

I am just fitting this next paragraph in because I have just driven to our local shops along one of the aforementioned roads. It seems some money has been found and they are starting to dig up the bad patches ready to fill with cement. The problem is that they have left hardly any room for cars to pass, and bigger vehicles have got no chance. Now if they had put signs at turn offs, warning vehicles to take another route, all would be well, but no, that is being far too organised. So large transport, driving from one direction will have to return at least 6 kilometres, because they can't get through. From the other direction it is even longer. It is always eventful on this road. On this trip I was chased by a pack of dogs, the leader kept up with my car for a remarkably long distance, snapping at my driver's door and giving me nasty looks. Further down the road after the yet to be filled in holes, there was a mule, who had obviously broken free from its tether, happily wandering down the road. I would have stopped, but what could I do with it, I could hardly tie it on the back of the car and crawl at a slow speed into town. I did think about parking up and riding it in, maybe someone would throw palm leaves in my path. Anyway I let it have its bit of freedom. It would spend a few leisurely hours amongst the olive trees, before one of the locals would recognise it and return it to the owner.

YO VIVO

A few years ago there was a competition to find a slogan and image to sum up what the Spanish mentality was all about. Keeping it in mind that only the Spanish could enter, the winning cartoon was of a little boy urinating in someone's doorway. I am trying to remember the slogan but it was something along the lines of "I Live; I will do what I want," the actual words were "Yo Vivo" (I live) I leave you to fathom that one out. The word mañana means tomorrow, but it has a far deeper significance. It is used to express an attitude of mind, a feeling about things not having to be done instantly. I suppose you could say it is akin to saying "Chill out, it will get done eventually." Now the idea that the Spanish here in the campo are laid back, "What will be, will be," is not exactly true. If it does not affect them directly, then it is always good for a gossip, but they don't really care. But if it does affect them, then the proverbial hits the fan. Denouncing, to the police, if not a national pastime, is certainly quite a popular course of action.

THE POLICE

Now here I have to watch what I am saying. Not because I fear any prosecution, but because like a lot of people, I think the standard of policing in these parts is shockingly bad, and I may just go overboard with my opinions. They are not really keen on all the paperwork involved in local rural crimes and tend to ignore minor grievances between individuals. My local little shop out here in the countryside was broken into four times before the police even came to take a look. Seven cave houses in this region have been broken into, and not one person has even been interviewed let alone arrested. Several livestock were rounded up and stolen; a local saw them, took the number plate of the vehicle and reported it. The police said "sorry we know the people they are gypsies, but as we did not see them do it, we can do nothing." A friend who was Rumanian was dragged from his car and beaten up, before being thrown in a cell. It turns out they were after his brother for a domestic complaint. They offered no apologies and denied hitting him; despite the fact he was limping and covered in bruises.

There are different types of police. Most villages have a local policeman, they tend to be nicer, because they have to live amongst us and life would be hell for them, if they got too difficult. The general police are somewhat constrained by procedures, but the Guardia are still basically army, and as such are not allowed to have a union. They are still seen as bullies, partly because they will never live down the period that they were Franco's police force. Part of their pay comes from fines, hence the proliferation of instant fines and gathering like vultures near roundabouts, to stop just about every car without pretext. On top of that they even announce in the press that they are going to increase the number of fines, not that more people are committing motoring offences. On the spot fines are the worst scenarios. I've had a friend frog marched to a cash machine, for not indicating at a junction. Look on line at the countless tourists that have been put in a situation where if they don't pay up, trumped up charges are added. I was driving slowly one morning and came up behind a police car, which was crawling along at a snail's pace. I hung back but one of the officers stuck his hand out of the window and waved me passed. I assumed they were waiting for someone, so I obeyed and was then promptly pulled over and fined 200 euros for overtaking them on a solid white line. I refused to pay, they wanted my credit card, but luckily I didn't have one, and only twenty euros in my pocket. I demanded an official docket which having no way of getting money from me they handed over, after I had taken a note of their registration number and told them my brother was an important lawyer (I don't have a brother) Six months later a letter came by post telling me that I was banned from driving for three months, from the date of the offence. In England I was stopped twice in thirty years, over here I have been stopped fourteen times in eight years, and none of them for obvious breeches of the law.

I have a Spanish friend who I won't name, but I am sure he won't mind me relating an incident. This friend has been known in the past to grow a little marijuana above the legal limit of three plants. It wasn't enough to run a business, but it was enough to supply a few of the local police with their requirements. One day a new boss arrived at the police station and decided to find out who has been supplying his men. One officer owned up, and my friend was issued with an ultimatum. Tell the new boss who else he supplies, and which officers are involved, and he will not be done. My friend does not like the police, but is still not prepared to split on them. The consequence was that he ended up doing six months in jail. He did not have a job, or any money and fairly soon they started chucking him out for odd days, I presume to save on costs. Sometimes he did not have the bus fare back home from the jail, which was over an hour's journey away. So he would sit in a bar with one beer all day, till they let him back in.

There is a Spanish word called 'Chivato' it was explained by a local language teacher to mean the general attitude of Spanish people towards Whistle-blowers. Now I know that rumour and suspicion abound everywhere, and telling on others is not always considered a good thing by some, i.e. honour amongst thieves or snitching to the boss for favour or jealousy. But in this country the person whistleblowing is often seen in a worse light than the perpetrator of the misdeed. If you can get something over on someone else, it is considered macho and almost praiseworthy. Hence the massive amount of corruption, that no one seemed to mind. However changing times and recent scandals, where the divide between the have and have not's has been graphically demonstrated, is starting to change general opinions.

BLOWING MY OWN TRUMPET

Well actually it's a saxophone, but the paragraph title was too good not to use. About fifteen years ago, and inspired by a friend of a friend who could blow some cool jazz and blues on the saxophone; I went out and spent far more money than I could afford at the time, on a second hand instrument. The shop keeper assured me it was one of the best makes you could buy. Actually he was right; it was just that the player was one of the worst students you could find. I honestly tried but after a year of driving my girlfriend mad, it kind of gathered dust in the corner. During the early rush of enthusiasm, I had even cleared out the gap under the stairs, put a door on it and padded it out with polystyrene sheets to stop the sound. This was to be my rehearsal space. Unfortunately it was only big enough for one chair and my music stand. The single light bulb, hanging from its chord, just inches above my head. Getting into position I asked my friend to shut the door. The first five minutes where reasonably fine, although the sound reverberated back on me from the panels, and I had to stuff a cloth down the horn end to stop it from deafening me. But then the heat from the bulb began to curl the receding hairs on my already thinning head. It also appeared to be getting generally very warm in the enclosed space. Now bearing in mind, that the light switch was outside, and my friend for a joke had wedged a chair against the door in response to my muffled complaint about the increasing heat. After a short time I abandoned trying to play and was shoving hard against the door and complaining loudly. Now my woodworking skills are no better than my saxophone playing abilities. After a couple of hearty shoves the two hinges on my now temporary door gave way and I collapsed through the opening ,holding my saxophone high to prevent damage and taking a blow to the other shoulder for my efforts.

So there it sat in its case for a year or so until it came to the time to decide exactly what I could pack into an old estate car, to start my new life in Spain. As it turned out a lot of what I took proved pointless, but for some reason the saxophone came with me, although I had a good chance to sell it and recoup some of my original expenditure. Once installed in Spain it sat for another three years in the new corner gathering Spanish dust. Then I moved to my new home and surprise, surprise the local village had a marching band. The initial interest from my point of view was not only to integrate myself, but they did a lot of socialising at festivals, and got paid, fed and watered generously. What I didn't realise was that I would be the only Brit in a fifty strong orchestra, and not a single one of them spoke more than a few words of English. This was not such a problem as in general they were quite welcoming, and I knew enough to exchange general banter. It was the rehearsals that turned out to be three times a week for two hours, which caused the problems. Firstly they could all read sheet music fluently or at least had been playing the incomprehensible Spanish marching stuff, since they were five years old. I have never seen so many notes on a page jammed together. They ran up and down the staves like musical diarrhoea. Most of the time I was frantically searching at least ten bars further back than the part they were playing. Desperate glances at the leader, who was conducting, usually went un-noticed, except for the odd frowned expression at me in the back row playing totally the wrong notes. In the end I just pretended to play, at least that way only my fellow saxophonists knew I was not contributing to the overall sound. One to one tuition was better; at least I had time to see what it is I was supposed to do. But once the band struck up, I was lost; they seemed to play everything at a hundred miles an hour.

I did make progress, but never enough to be allowed to actually march and play with them when they performed. That was actually a blessing, because my sense of rhythm which is not too bad from the waste up, cannot be said for my legs. In rehearsals I would slowly be left behind, as we marched around the hall. Well what do you expect? You have to read the music which is clipped to a small plate that is screwed into the body of the saxophone. It is placed exactly in line and behind the main stem, so you have to lean slightly sideways, or go completely boss eyed to read it. Even then the notes are tiny, and I didn't understand them anyway. I suspect that most of them had never come into much contact with an English man before, I could imagine what they must have been thinking, if I was their only example of my race. Despite their patience, it became a nightmare and I had to find a face saving way of leaving. Breaking my leg and having eight screws and a plate fitted, left me with a serious permanent limp. But I would have preferred to have found a less painful solution. After that I found a teacher of jazz and blues; this was much more to my liking. Nowadays I still play infrequently and am involved with music playing guitar and piano. I will never be very good at any of them, but it gives me pleasure.

I have to add one last thing about my saxophone. Last year I was struggling to pay a large repair bill for my car and decided to sell a few musical items. These consisted of a couple of amplifiers and an old guitar I did not use. I also decided it was time for the saxophone to go. A friend purchased it, but I knew that he was never likely to play it. My intuition was correct, because he did not intend to learn. A short time later, he gave it back to me as a gift, saying that no musician should be forced to sell his instruments. I know that a couple of my friends had shared the initial purchase cost, but I never found out exactly who. Rather than offer to lend me money, which I would have refused, they hatched this kind plan. It still brings a tear to the eye when I think about it.

And so the Saxophone stays with me through thick and thin, I really must try once again to make my friend's generous gesture worthwhile.

WOODROT

It started off as a small group of friends meeting to strum and blow or bang a collection of instruments. None of us had the slightest intention of playing in public; mind you I doubt any audience would have stayed long if we had. However over time we got a little braver and suggestions were made that we found a bar and started playing in the corner. We could invite others to join us. This took place and a young rock guitarist and another two singers joined our little group. It was the beginning of an attempt to form a band, in fact two bands. The genesis of people who had originally met to strum became THE PLONKERS and the band including a rock guitarist became the HOWLERS. I think there are still videos of us on YouTube, but I would not advise trying to find them.

It was a casual idea five years ago to have a picnic outside during the summer and invite anyone we knew who could play any instrument or sing, to come along and join in with a jam session. As with ideas discussed amongst friends, it got more and more grandiose as we thought about it. By the time a day had been decided, we were talking about camping areas, portable toilets and even a stage and P.A. equipment. It was already a long way from a bottle of pop and a few sandwiches, whilst someone strummed old Donovan numbers.

As I have quite a lot of open land, we cleared a slope for people to sit on, admittedly it was a little steep and various items including bodies kept sliding down the hill. The stage was constructed by hanging green windbreak material over some poles. The musicians consisted of friends who could knock out a tune. We did try to get a couple of locals that were considered at least semi-professional, but they gracefully declined. I remember thinking if not saying; you wait till it's as big as Glastonbury or Woodstock, and then see if we will let you play. And that's when we came up with the name, it was officially called Woodrot. Having temporarily converted my outbuilding into a unisex toilet and plastered posters in all the local shops, I waited with bated breath to see who would come. The start time was 3pm if I remember and by two on a very hot Saturday, there were a few friends and that was all. Then slowly cars began to arrive and I spent the next hour rushing around trying to sort out bad parking, places for people to pitch their ten men, all-purpose conference tents, including barbeque area. Then a giant camper van half the size of my house turned up, followed by several slightly smaller versions. It reminded me of a mother and her chicks. I can see why Michael Eavis recently got knighted or something; I had totally underestimated what was needed to run an event. By 3.30 there were about 150 people setting out their picnics, constructing sun shades and trying to stop their bowls of salad and chicken portions from rolling down the slope.

Despite the bad planning and the local police snooping around asking me if I had started a campsite business, it turned out to be a great day and night. I told the officer that it was my birthday party. In Spanish he replied "Blimey, you've got a lot of friends!" People were saying they could not wait for the next one; I on the other hand had not slept for at least 48 hours and was emotionally strung out. When my head finally hit the pillow it stayed in that position for a long time. Meanwhile outside people were staggering from their tents and frying breakfasts.

Spurred on by the success of the first one, we had Woodrot 2 a year later. This time we had a metal flatbed trailer for the stage and rather hastily built block toilets, with personal hanging toilet rolls on string. I had also cut three terraces in the banking so that the audience could sit and eat on the level. This was much appreciated by those who got a little drunk the year before and ended up at the foot of the hill, every time they tried to go anywhere.

We invited anyone and everyone to come and play and ended up with six bands and numerous solo singers. Four of the groups were Spanish Rock Bands and the P.A. being a lot louder, they could hear us right across the valley. We had a real bar and a friend ran a great homemade food stall, it was so popular, she had to rush home to make more. The whole event lasted into the early hours of the morning and was much more of a mixed cultural event. I could see this starting to become something big in the local calendar. At a rough head count, I estimated over three hundred people attended, double the previous year's figures. It was a good event apart from the fact I was hobbling with a crutch, recovering from my broken leg. The only other incident that enlivened the night was when someone who had a bit too much to drink fell into one of the girl singers. The drummer, threw down his sticks, leapt over his drum set and assaulted the drunk. It kind of put an end to their set.

Then came Woodrot 3, I knew our luck would not hold out. Firstly the other two previous events had taken place in perfect sunny conditions, if not a little too hot. This time we had just had six weeks without rain, and after the event would have another month or so of dry weather, but yes you have guessed it. For three days only, we had storms and torrential rain. Not that it started that way. The morning of the event was sunny, we erected a magnificent awning and speaker stacks that we had made, and it looked just like the professional thing. On top of that we had built a permanent concrete stage and even obtained a proper temporary loo with running water and flush system. For the first time it looked like we had planned well, there was a website offering directions, performer information and flashy posters. It started with an hour of music in slowly worsening conditions. First came the clouds and the sun disappeared, followed by gusts of wind that grew in intensity. I have a bit of video of a friend singing into a microphone, she is leaning at an impossible angle to prevent being swept away. Then the rain came, little drops, then bigger drops, and finally the full package, hammering down on the brave few that had not retreated to the safety of their cars. The stage became a river, collecting all the water running down from the viewing slope, and it became obvious that it was going to ruin expensive equipment and possibly cause someone to be electrocuted. We had no option but to abandon the event, bearing in mind our average audience age was nearer fifty than the wet, mud loving twenty something's of other music festivals.

It was then I suggested over the P.A. that rather than going home, everyone moved inside, into my cave house system. This was a bit rash but born out of desperation, after so much work and planning, I hated losing. Luckily quite a lot of people had read the weather forecast and not come, but there were still over a hundred people crammed into my cave rooms. At first it was chaos, there was hardly room to move. Several friends were soaked to the skin, taking down the sound system, before it was ruined and there were a lot of performers who had not even had a chance to play, some had come a long way. I ushered musicians into different cave rooms and told them to make the best of it, set themselves up at one end and just start playing. It turned into a magic party; you could squeeze yourself from one room to another and hear different live music in each. It was like several

Liverpool cavern clubs rolled into one. If it had been arranged this way, it may not have worked. People would have complained about lack of space, claustrophobia or whatever, but because we were all in the same boat, everyone was smiling and having a good time. I did not tell them, but one old sofa was the normal bed of three dogs and a cat, not exactly hygienic, and I would never sit on it. But why spoil their fun, the room had subdued lighting, and they could brush all the hairs of their trousers in the morning.

Again I had the police, this time in plain clothes, trying to find if I was selling anything illegal or without the correct licences. As by that time we had all moved indoors, I kept them outside in the rain and told them it was a private party on my property. They annoyed me because all the local village fiestas are un- regulated, have large fires for their paellas, when it is forbidden to light fires in the summer. Then they let off dozens of rockets throughout the day, all of which land in the dry grass, but the police turn a blind eye. However as we are not Spanish, it seems we are fair game.

It continues to grow; Woodrot 4 has now come and gone. It took place in a large tent in the middle of the local village. It had English and Spanish singers and bands, a large PA system, and full backing of the town mayor. But the character kind of changed, after moving from my field. Planning for the next one is underway but I have retired, it could well develop into a tradition for the village.

FLAMENCO

Fired with enthusiasm at hearing an amazing, but unknown guitarist playing flamenco at a hundred miles an hour in the tourist parts of Granada, I decided that I would teach myself to play this style of music. It was not very long before I realised that my fingers were not capable of doing the sort of gymnastics required, and certainly not at those speeds. In the end I did manage to compose my one and only bit, of very slow Spanish sounding music. After that I went back to my rock and roll. There are several styles of Flamenco music, characterised by deep and profound lyrics and developed originally by the Gitanos (Gypsies), mostly in the Andalucía region. Back in the 18th century the gypsies were also called Flamencos, hence the link. Apparently they were more interested in passing on emotions and feelings through music rather than writing. This led to what is often termed "Duende" It is a way to express moments when passion from the performer, is empathically transferred to the audience. It does not happen all the time, just at moments when everyone present, shares a common emotion. The original Gitanos, who started inhabiting southern Spain after the expulsion of the Moors by the Christians, had a very tough life, living mostly off the beaten track and hand to mouth. Guitars were possibly not widely owned, so the rhythms were beaten out by hand clapping. This is still part of the traditional accompaniment to flamenco playing and dancing to this day .The styles are known as "Palos" some adhere rigidly to a tradition whilst others are more freely interpreted. There are over fifty different forms, but these days only a dozen or so are regularly performed. For you music buffs out there, most are based on a twelve or four beat pattern. The Cante Jondo, are the serious styles with traces of Spanish, Moorish, Byzantine, Christian and Jewish religious music incorporated. Cante Chico is more light hearted and humorous. The rest, lie somewhere between. Some of the names such as Fandango, Bulerias and Tango will be familiar to you, but there are many more with names such as Farruca, Siguiriyas and Guajiras. Granada is the city to go to around here, if you want to hear Flamenco. The old Gypsy quarter on the hill overlooking the Alhambra palace, is the place to listen to very accomplished players and singers, who earn from playing on the street. Unfortunately for them, in a country of flamenco guitarists, you have to be incredible to rise above the majority.

OLIVES, ALMONDS, ADVOCADOS, CHIRIMOYA and WINE

You can't talk about this area of Spain without talking about olives, it has more olive trees than any other country, something in the order of 300 million (about 5.19 million acres) and is still the world's largest exporter although rivals are gaining fast as the older generation dies off, and the youngsters are not so keen to take over. The oil is used not only in cooking but to fuel lamps, as preservatives, medicine, cosmetics and even as a laxative.

Olive trees grow very slowly and originally only produced fruit after about fifteen years, modern techniques have shortened this to just five years. The olive tree is at its best after 40 years and will continue to produce until it is in the region of 140 years old. However there are examples of olive trees that are well over a thousand years old, planted back in Visigoth and Arab times. Each olive only releases a few drops of oil, it would take 11 kilos of them to produce one kilo of oil. Everything is ground into a pulp, then spun centrifugally, which brings the aceite to the surface, then it is filtered to get rid of water and any impurities. The best oil is the extra virgin which is basically the very first pressing, which still contains most of the vitamins. The normal term for the olive is aceituna and the oil is called Aceite de Oliva, to distinguish it from engine oil.

The history of the olive in Spain dates back some 6000 years, but it is the Romans who really started to use it in quantity. Mount Testaccio in Italy, is made up of approximately 40 million amphorae (oil containers) discarded during a period of 250 years. Hadrian had a coin minted with an olive branch on it and the word "Hispania"

When in later times Catholic fundamentalism took over the country, olive production fell into decline. It was all because of pigs and pork becoming a sure sign of faith in a land full of heathen Jews and Moors. In its place pork lard took over and only the poor and destitute used olive oil which was then seen as a desperate substitute. In more recent times the government desperate for money sold vast quantities of olive oil to America and replaced it with Soya oil. Vast acres of ancient olives were ripped up and replaced with this new crop. Luckily wisdom prevailed and Olive production finally started to thrive again in the late seventies, although a lot was sold cheaply to Italy, who re labelled it and sold it on at much higher prices. Now everything is controlled by the Denominacion de Origin system, similar to the wines in France.

The traditional way to harvest the olives is to beat the life out of the tree with a long stick, it is very tiring work, I know because my Spanish friend forced me to help him. You lay large nets under each tree and proceed to fill it, before dragging the very heavy material over to a flatbed trailer and then do your back in, trying to heave the olives into it. When you look up and see rows of the sodding things stretching into the far distance, you suddenly loose complete interest in the rural life, and wish you still had that cushy office job. There were four of us and by the end of the third day I was proudly the only one left standing. The Rumanian had broken his ankle falling down a bank, my friend's wife had decided enough was enough, it was man's work, and my friend had literally put his back out. Recently I have seen the big local Olive growers use what looks like a giant inverted umbrella that fits around the tree to collect the olives. Then a tractor with clamps on it embraces the tree shaking it violently to free all the olives.

The old locals look on disapprovingly, muttering that it disturbs the roots, and will shorten the life of the tree.

Almonds

Almonds are the next biggest crop in this region, for most of the year the trees look dead, almost like the bark has been scorched by fire. It is only when they burst into bloom that they suddenly come alive and look spectacular. Traditionally the locals would do the "Dance of the Almonds," separating the skins from the shells by smashing the fruit with their feet, but I assume they use machines now. It has been a major crop in Andalucía for at least a thousand years. The story goes that that a Moorish Caliph, planted almonds all around the hills of Cordoba , then called Mecca, as a gift to his wife. Spain stands second to California as the largest growing centre in the world. Like the Olives, the almonds are knocked down with sticks or just left to fall naturally. It is only the frost and freezing weather that can ruin them. October is the month that they harvest in Andalucía. In my previous village there was an antiquated machine that had flywheels, rubber belts and a noisy petrol engine. The locals would drag it out at the appropriate time of year and feed bag after bag of almonds into the hopper. Slowly the air would fill up with fine dust and two piles would form on the ground. One was the husks and the other the nice shelled nuts. I always assumed that the husks were not good for much, but in fact they are almost as valuable as the almonds. Many people around here use almond burners instead of log fuelled stoves. The older versions included a mini hopper at the top, whilst underneath it fed a box furnace. They can be tricky to use and many a person has been smoked out of the room, but if you get it right, they are a cheap way to heat your house. The sack of husks don't take up as much room as a giant pile of Olive fire wood, but you still need a suitable storage area for them. The newer versions are all trendy, but I have noticed that the fans they use are generally very noisy, not easy to sit and relax next too. I prefer the old versions, much more pleasing and rustic.

Advocados

Avocadoes grow nearer the coast in Andalucía, my area is too high and cold for them, they can't tolerate lower than minus one degree centigrade. I really love the taste; there is nothing better with fresh tomatoes and a dash of extra virgin olive oil, washed down with some nice red wine. The trees can grow to twenty meters tall, and the fruit can be the size of your clenched fist. The ones I can buy in the supermarket here are pathetic scrawny examples, but if I am willing to drive two hours down to the coast to my friend's orchard, I can return with bucket loads of big fat ones. That gives me an idea to make a bit of cash on the side. It is best to get them hard, and then wait a week or two till you can start to feel them give under the pressure of your thumb. Once ripened, they will go off very quickly, and become much darker in colour. I have also picked them with friends, the lower branches are easy, but these trees can grow very high. If you hang on to the half-filled bucket with one hand, whilst pulling the fruit with a quick tug with the other hand, what is holding you in position on that branch?

Cherimoya

Cherimoya is a weird looking fruit, which only grows down near the Mediterranean coast of Andalucía. It looks a bit like a space probe, or a hand grenade with strange hexagonal panels. We had a lot where I used to live, but one cold frost killed them all, we had to rip them up and start again. Mark Twain called it the "most delicious fruit to men" but I am not so sure, it is quite a strange taste something between several other fruits and to me it is a bit like eating cream and sultanas with a mere hint of pepper. Its nickname is custard apple and is described in the dictionary as a blend of banana, pineapple, papaya, peach and strawberry. People either love it or hate it. I also find it quite hard to prepare. You can't just bite into it unless you want a mouthful of very large pips. It takes an expert, or a very patient person to scrape off the eatable paste from them.

Wine

You can't talk about Spain, without mentioning wine. The best thing for me is that I can go into my local shop and pay the equivalent of two pounds, and walk out with a bottle of red wine that would cost at the very least eight pounds in England. It is very tempting to over indulge, and have it with nearly every meal, unlike the beer here, which is crap. I have a friend who gets through almost two bottles of wine a day on his own, but that is another story. The best bottle I ever tasted was purchased in a tiny village shop for 95 cents (about 70 pence) It was so good I ran back and brought the lot that they had, it was called something terrible like "lightning" but I can't remember exactly. Unfortunately they never had it again, and I haven't seen it anywhere since. The locals harvest their own grapes and produce some seriously powerful stuff that can be purchased in five litre plastic containers. It is not treated with preservatives, so will go off fairy quickly when exposed to air. That means you have to invite a lot of friends around, or get totally plastered on your own. You don't see many men drinking wine in the bars, it is always beer, but according to statistics the average Spanish person downs 21.6 litres a year, actually that doesn't sound so much, that's not even two litres a month.

2.9 million acres are planted in Spain, which makes it the largest growing area in the world, but due to the spacing of the trees, it is only third on the list for production, behind France and Italy. The best Spanish red wine for me is a good Rioja; you can't beat it, although Ernest Hemingway, that writer who was just a little better than me at writing, (Ha!) liked Valdepenas.

Grapes were first cultivated sometime between 4000 and 3000 BC, although it was the Romans in1100 BC, who started exporting it around their empires. Ovid wrote that not all the wines were good, one popular Spanish wine sold in Rome, known as *Saguntum* was only good for getting your mistress drunk. It was Christopher Columbus discovering the new world and then Conquistadors and Missionaries that took grape saplings to the new world. Californian wine has them to thank for that. There are 79 Quality Wine areas across Spain and a quality control system called Denomination de Origen Calificada. However only two areas at present qualify by being consistently of a high quality, these are Rioja and Priorat.

There is also Vin de Mesa, wines that are the equivalent of table wines and are made from unclassified vineyards or grapes that have been declassified through blending. Jerez produces a Sherry, and in Cataluña they have developed Cava, better known as poor man's Champagne. I once got very drunk on what the shepherd, who was imbibing with me, called local Mosto. The official description says it is grape juice, before it is finally processed as wine. It still has the pulpy mass of seeds in it and is not totally fermented. I like the dictionary description ,which said it is an experimentation of diverse elements. But what I can guarantee is that two glasses of the stuff I had, was enough to blow my socks off, and I didn't remember very much of the rest of the day.

Pollard stumps near Benamaurel

POST

The postal system in these outlying settlements is interesting. My village which now contains only a few people, once had a couple of hundred. In its centre is a wall with small metal post-boxes. All of them are now unused, and all of them are damaged. It is the same in the next small Pueblo and I presume a lot of others. The easiest way to get our mail is to collect in from the post office in the nearest larger village. I don't know what happened in the past, but our local postman has been banished to an up and over garage on the outskirts of town. He has done his best by installing a proper window and door at the front, but it is still in the middle of a row of grey metal folding doors. I bet it is cold in winter; he is a nice man and doesn't deserve to spend his life in a concrete garage.

Most of my post is from business and friends and as such bears my proper name. But it is not the case for official Spanish letters from the Council, Hospital, and Police etc. My full name is John Simpson Moody, the middle name being my mother's maiden name. This in itself promotes hilarity when it is spoken, as they are well into the Simpsons cartoon series over here. No one has dared calling me Homer yet, but I am just waiting. Last week I received a letter addressed to Jhou Slimson Modi; the nice postman actually drove out and handed it to me. Deviating just slightly, my friends surname is Porro, it means Spliff. (For those of you who are still innocent, it is slang for a joint, cigarette with marijuana) The police find it particularly amusing; after they have realised he is not trying to be sarcastic with them. Anyway back to the subject on hand.

Generally a Spanish name will have the father's name after the first name, followed by other family names, possibly including the mother's name. So if someone was called Antonio Gonzalez Carranza, the Gonzalez would be his father's name. Thus everyone thinks I am Mr Simpson. I have forgotten how many times in offices I have had to explain that the British put the male name last. They still call me Senor Simpson and most local letters arrive addressed to my alter- ego.

It tends to fall to the first Brit who enters the post office on any given day, to take all the mail for any other ex-pat that lives within ten miles of them.

Old Olive stump

MY CATS THINK THEY ARE DOGS

In the beginning there were two tiny abandoned kittens, so small that you could hold them in the palm of one hand, their eyes not even open. Later after much care and attention these two tiny cats were strong enough to hang on to my friends jeans as he attempted to paint a wall, causing him to laugh and cry at the same moment as their little claws sunk into his skin. Down the line and two years later two powerful Tom cat's patrol my garden, not exactly in love with each other anymore, but willing to share the patch, providing their individual food bowls remain sacrosanct.

Rodrigo and Pablo, although more often than not now referred to as Stompy and Nudge for reasons I will explain shortly, have complete control over my three very large dogs.(now five) As the two cats firmly believe they are dogs, despite the difference in size, they have absolutely no fear of any visiting animals. Friend's dogs have two choices; they can wag their tails and lick the cat's on the face, in which case they are allowed in to sit quietly with everyone, or they can growl or worse still attempt to chase one of them. If this happens the dog is best getting out of there as fast as he can. It is the only time that my two cats will side with each other, and like a pair of sheep dogs will herd the offending animal into a corner before launching a combined attack.

Stompy is far too fat, I think he has several sources of food other than the meals I provide. When he walks it is like watching an old pugilist approaching from the other side of the ring, hence the nickname. Pablo on the other hand is all sweetness and light until roused. He will nuzzle and nudge you all day for affection and likes nothing better than lying around your neck whilst you are watching television, or on the computer. He won't even move if you get up to make a cup of tea. He is no lightweight either, so after a while the old neck begins to ache, and he is most put out when you suggest enough is enough.

Living way out in the countryside in Spain it is not always easy to get to a vet. When the time came for them to be sterilised, I thought it easier if the travelling vet came out to me. She arrived in a battered old van, a hard, scruffy blunt talking middle aged woman. I think her first words to me went along the lines of.

'Bloody;.,#~@#' you live in a :~#~ difficult place to find, Hope you got them cat's ready, I'm behind with my visits , next woman has twelve cat's to see too, what the F@:}}{~ does she want twelve for? We can do it out here on your window sill!

Those of you especially males with a delicate disposition should miss out the rest of this paragraph. Basically she pinned each cat in turn in the corner of its cat cage with a clever wire grid thing, before putting each temporarily to sleep. Each cat in turn was laid on the sill, its ball sacks slit open and with a rough yank each ball was ripped out. It took less than twenty seconds a cat. She said a rip was better than a sharp cut, because it healed quicker, having rough edges.

And that was it, apart from her wanting to include me in a 3 for the price of 2 offer! Feeling slightly feint I declined the invitation. Within a day both cats were back to normal, squabbling with each other and wondering why something appeared to be missing at the other end.

When the dogs line up for their food, so do the two cats. When someone is at the gate, faced through the wire by an Alsatian a Doberman type and a large shaggy werewolf (softest of the lot) there are also often two cats sitting staring at them as well. The only difference is that the cats can get on your lap, mind you come to think of it the werewolf tries from time to time.

In fact this isn't a story at all, more a collection of incidents, the first happened when they were still quite young. Pablo went missing and after a couple of days I started searching around the locality. There are no other buildings near me, just a lot of Olive trees and barren slopes. Not far from my home was a set of very tall narrow trees stretching sixty foot up, they are often cut to make poles. And being thin they wave in a big arc when the wind blows. There was the faintest of cries but I heard it and looking up, I could just make out the shape of a tiny cat wedged in one of the topmost branches. Even if the tree could have withstood my sixteen stone weight, at my age it would have been a suicide mission, so I phoned a friend. Ben was a young lad that liked what they call free running (they jump off buildings) it appealed to his sense of adventure and he volunteered readily to climb up and affect a rescue. Wearing leather gloves, and a rucksack for storing a frightened cat on his back, he ascended in much the same manner as my cat must have, in other words quickly. I just chickened out and closed my eyes, wondering if my house insurance covered falling friends. After two days up there the cat was not going to readily let go of its branch, and through peeping fingers I watched the lad with his legs entwined around what was an incredibly thin branch that was swaying disturbingly, trying to prize the cat away from its security. Finally he managed to yank it free but then had the problem of getting the rucksack off his back and popping a squirming cat with sharp claws into it. Drop the animal and even a cat would be lucky to survive such a drop. Somehow he did it, I didn't see because by then I had really chickened out, and was busy inspecting a stone on the floor. My friend came down slightly slower with a visibly moving rucksack on his back. Ten feet from the bottom, the cat squirmed out and shot to the ground before running off. An hour later I was inspecting the scratches on my friends back where Pablo had penetrated the rucksack and his jacket. The cat walked in as calm as you like and sat looking at its food bowl.

Being a sucker for animals I have provided my dogs with a couple of old sofas to sleep on. All worked well for a month or so, the cats had their own secret places to sleep. Then one morning I came out of my bedroom to be confronted by three very sheepish and miserable looking dogs. Normally they are full of enthusiasm to see me. At first I thought that they had done something like destroying my shoes or ripping open a rubbish bag. The week before one or more of them had managed to reduce two plastic dog bowls to a pile of shards. However I found nothing and promptly forgot about it. After the second morning I decided to investigate and getting out of bed quietly at some ungodly hour I opened the door quickly. All three dogs were huddled together on the cold stone floor instead of their sofas. Moving over, it became apparent what the problem was, one cat per sofa, none of us were brave enough to try and shift them that night.

These two are the first cats I have ever had, being basically a dog man. Not only giving two helpless kittens a chance, but also the thought that they may one day repay me by catching a few mice. However I am slowly coming to understand these creatures. Yes they can be aloof, have their own agendas and treat you like a servant, but they bring a different kind of friendship to my home and I would not be without them now. Pablo is keeping my lap nice and warm whilst I type this.

I have at the moment three, very large, and two medium dogs; they spend most of the day sitting in the sun outside my Spanish cave home, waiting for the next meal time. The only useful job they do is to bark at the occasional unfortunate stranger who wanders our way. Why do I mention this, well because I am jealous, I have to work to earn enough to pay their large food bills, I just get beans on toast.

Last week my local supermarket made me an offer I could not refuse. If I purchased three large cans of dog meat they would give me completely free of charge, a dog collar. As the neck size of my brutes, needed one twice as long as the small red ones they had, I asked if I could buy six cans and get two collars that I would then join together. Obviously I was just trying to be funny, but it did not translate as a joke, because the Spanish lady behind the counter took me very seriously and spent ten minutes explaining that it just would not work. I just let her finish and left collarless. Now if the promotional collars had been suitable I would have stockpiled them until I had enough, but as she could not confirm that there would be further supplies, I figure the dog food company missed out on a valuable client. Well actually in thinking about it, they didn't, I have to buy the damn stuff anyway.

I had friends who came for a holiday and as a thank you for letting them stay in my unique home they left behind three big sacks of dog biscuits and twenty tins of meat. It lasted just three weeks, no wonder I am always broke.

Dedicated

I don't understand why the authorities don't do more about the strays. It would be so much more kind on all the starving dogs roaming around .This book is dedicated to all the dogs I have looked after since I came to Spain .They were all strays and came to me in a variety of ways and conditions, this is just a list of happy and sad memories.

Sombre A podenco who was found abandoned under a car in the rain as a little pup. She grew to be a big tall rangy dog with a sweet but nervous nature. One day she ran off and never came back. That is the worst sensation, not knowing what happened to her.

Possum My favourite dog of all in Spain. Someone had cut her ears and tail off roughly. She was the strangest dog I have ever seen, short curly hair and eyes of different colours, she didn't even run like a dog, but she did look like a possum. Very independent and leader of the pack, she knew she was special. She died of heat stroke and I will always blame myself because I could have prevented it.

Tich hung around my gate for days slowly getting braver. Poor little soul, he had a really bad eye infection which was caused by leishmaniasis, slowly the infection spread to his paws ,nose and other parts. We fought hard for almost a year and he was very stoical with his special homemade eye patch, but in the end it was so bad, he had to be put to sleep.

PeeWee came with me when we moved here from the coast. He was a street dog that decided to move up in the world. He loved being cuddled and held in your arms. Died very quickly, of a heart attack one evening.

Paws was a beautiful Dalmatian, found hiding under a wood pile and refused to come out for ages. I left my hand dangling by his nose and eventually he started licking it. Paws loved sleeping on the sofa. One day he came rushing out of the bushes panic stricken, something was wrong and I rushed him to the vets, but half way there he died whilst licking my hand again. We think he was bitten by a snake, or ate some poison put down by the local chicken farm to kill foxes.

Snowy. I found Snowy dying of starvation on the hill above my land, he was all skin and bones and did not move, and in fact I thought he was dead at first. He could not even get up, so I put a blanket around him and left food and water near his mouth. In the morning the food was gone and he attempted to get up, but still could not. I built him a kennel just where he lay, and after a few days kept moving the food a little further away. Within the month he was staggering around on very wobbly legs. Eventually I moved him into the house with the others and he put on weight, but never played with them. He always looked sad and lost, but I had hopes. Things were improving when after six months he suddenly fell ill. The vet said he needed to operate because it was peritonitis. Snowy fought hard to resist the anaesthetic, because I think he knew. He died on the operating table.

Obi the Alsatian is the longest surviving dog I have. She is getting old now and her back legs are starting to give her problems. She follows me everywhere and sits guarding my bedroom door at night. Obi loves being hovered with the vacuum cleaner. She used to be a stray begging for food outside a bar. Her trick was to get under the table and wag her tail furiously until someone gave her some attention. Obi waited outside my door one day and refused to go away. Recently she has been having a lot of problems with leaking. I took her to the vet who did an ex-ray. It turns out that she is full of Calcium deposits. No more tap water for us from now on, just bottled water.

Sienna is a Doberman cross mongrel, who just likes to stare into your eyes. She is very disobedient always trying to escape, but just as eager for forgiveness. A friend phoned to say that a puppy was hanging around his house, could I take it. Puppy my foot, Sienna came up to my knees and she was only about six months old. She likes barking at the slightest noise, especially in the middle of the night.

Tich2 A cheeky little white male mongrel with a cute face that turned up one day and would not leave. He is a master at escaping, and if he can take Sienna with him, all the better. They return from their adventures after a couple of hours, as if nothing had happened. I see them ambling up the track, tails wagging. He loves to play fight the other dogs who are all female and a lot larger than him. He just enjoys being beaten up by them, When one dog has grown tired of the game, Tich starts to agitate one of the others. My biggest dog Ruby is a shaggy monster, at least ten times bigger than Tich. They have an old sofa to play and sleep on. It is a hollow box construction under the padded seats. On two occasions I have heard Tich squeaking, but could not see him. Ruby would be sitting covering most of the sofa and looking innocent. Somehow they had been mock fighting and Ruby had sat on Tich, popping him down the back of the sofa and into the compartment below. You could see the moving bump in the material as the small dog looked for a way out.

Ruby is massive; she is just like one of the wild pigs that roam around here, wobbling along. I am sure one day a local farmer will take a pot shot at her. She is a big softy who will hide if you shout boo. You cannot but love Ruby, she is so cuddly and happy to play and be stroked. I took her in after a phone call from a friend, and nearly had a fit when they pushed this mountain of a dog out of the car. She was a twin, both of them originally roamed wild around the village I used to live in. Unfortunately her sister was hit by a car and died.

Bouncy. I have already mentioned Bouncy in this book, he was a fun loving little dog, that literally bounced around. We think he was attacked by wild pigs, but will never really know, he just vanished.

Chico Dumped on me after doing a favour and temporarily looking after him. Chico was moved around various foster homes and once dug himself out of a cave where he had been shut in. Very nervous and always wanting attention, but he now has a permanent home with me, and will learn to relax.

Asleep on my chair

SPANISH EXERCISE

It has long been a custom in most villages at least in this region to wander out at night in groups along the byways around the village. It is a time to chat and do a little exercise. When I first came here apart from the near naked runner, who turned out to be German, there did not seem to be an emphasis on straining oneself. It was all done at a slow amble. The groups might split up into sub sections, depending on age and ability, but there was certainly no rushing about. The normal time was around dusk, but I don't know if this was before or after settling down to a big meal. On one specific day each year, my old village would do a circuit around the outermost perimeter. It would start with the very young and their parents, and a bit later the other adults and youngsters, followed by teenagers and anyone else who wanted to make a lot of noise whilst doing it.

Lately I have seen a change in general trends. People are out in ones and two's and not just at dusk, but early in the morning. The gentle stroll has been replaced by gritted determination. We are not talking fit young people here, they do their own things running or on mountain bikes. The ones striding out tend to be mostly women of middle to more mature age. Body shapes vary, although a lot do look like they are in need of an exercise regime. This trend is growing rapidly and the good thing is, it is a healthy one.

More older men seem to be joining them of late, including two local guys who must be well into their eighties, who with several dogs, walk from the nearest pueblo to just up the lane from me, then back again. It has to be all of 8 klm, and they do it day after day, without stopping for rain or blazing sun. Another old guy always wears smart office trousers tucked into his socks and sometimes even a tie, as he strides along the road each day. Now that's what I call being an individual.

Out here in the countryside there is so little traffic, that you tend to notice when someone or something goes past. Mostly it is the odd car heading for a finca or towing various building materials, or olive cuttings in a noisy steel trailer that bounces along the unmade tracks. Then you get the local shepherd with his flocks of scrawny animals that are sometimes hard to decipher if they are sheep or goats. Their dogs are not the smart black and white collies we are used to seeing on the green hills of Britain. They tend to be scruffy, flea bitten mongrels that are more or less the same parched brown of the landscape. However they do know their job and chase around snapping at the heels of the flock. On one occasion I drove up behind them whilst they were all blocking the road and depositing millions on little neat balls of waste across the tarmac. The Shepherd, who was at the front, sent one of his dog's back to clear a path for me, through the herd. The dog was brilliant, it split the first section of the flock neatly in two, herding them to each side of the road and trotted in front of my car as we eased forward, parting the rest like Moses.

At the weekends we get all the earnest exercisers , a few striding out with those ridiculously long walking sticks that are meant to motivate you into covering vast distances at a pace, not much less than marathon walkers. However mostly it is the cyclists kitted out in luminous tight fitting outfits covered in brand names and trying to emulate their heroes from the Vuelta de Espana. Around here it tends to be more mountain bikes than road racing machines that would not last too long on these surfaces. Now I know I should not mock, but that is what this book is all about, so why not. The overweight ones should really not wear lycra, it does not become them, better a baggy tracksuit, until some of the bulk has gone. And what happens when most of them reach any sort of incline? The gearing becomes so ludicrously low that the little legs are spinning at an incredible rate, but very little progress is being made. I admire the ones who admit defeat and get off and push, at least they are being honest with themselves.

I am sometimes treated to the roar of a dozen or so motocross bikes, over-revving their way up and down the local terrain. This is not really exercise, although I should imagine the old arms take a pounding from the vibration and suspension shock. The track to my cave house used to continue past and connect to other rutted lanes. When I put a fence up it confused one hapless rider, who unlike Steve McQueen was not able to jump it, and so skidded straight into it. After picking himself up he made some comment about it not being there the last time he came this way.

We also get the ancient jeep convoy and even on one special day, a whole line of Skoda's. But the biggest groups are always the weekend motor bikers. Most of them are born again bikers, on large Harley Davidson copies, and the occasional genuine one. Clad from head to foot in black leather and space age helmets, despite it being a roasting hot day, they are more sedate than the motocross lads, as they cruise along following someone who thinks they know where they are going. Ten minutes later they cruise past again, after finding that the road is a dead end.

Lastly we get the large camper vans, mostly driven by grey haired men whilst their wife is trying to read an oversized map. I am lucky to have a large man-made lake not far from my home. It was made when the council flooded the valley some years back. However any map over a few years old still shows the road that is now lost deep in the murky waters. It looks the most obvious and direct route to cut off a long detour, if you are heading north. It has fooled many unwary travellers, who all seem to eventually end up outside my home, puzzling over what to do next. I usually wait till they have struggled through a few phrases of halting holiday Spanish, before replying in my best BBC accent, "Yes old boy, Madrid is that way."

Once a camper-van stopped and the man got out, I waited for the usual question, but was wondering why he appeared to be covered in quite a bit of wet mud.

"Excuse me, but can you help, there is a sheep stuck in the stream and now, so is my wife."

I saw that he was distressed so did not play my usual trick, and within two minutes we were down by the stream. Normally it is fairly slow running, but there had been some heavy rain the previous week, and now it would take your feet from under you if you ventured to mid-stream. The animal was caught by its back leg, trapped by a twisted branch. Its whole body was underwater and was only managing to keep its head up, because the brave lady was knee deep in the cold water holding it. We both waded in and he took over her job, whilst I tried to free the leg, luckily it was not as difficult as it first seemed, but then the animal began to struggle. I don't know how much it weighed but its coat was absolutely full of water and it took all three of us to even haul it partially onto the bank, where it lay exhausted. After a rest, and some of the water had drained from its coat, we managed to pull it fully clear. It must have been struggling for some time because, even after we had retired to my home and cleaned up, then returned, it had not moved. I informed the Shepherd and the next day it was gone, one way or the other. That is now the third animal I have pulled out of that river.

WILDLIFE

We seem to have deviated from exercise to animals again, so I may as well tell you about the other wild life around here. We have wild pigs called jabali; these are not to be tampered with and have been known to kill people from time to time. The local hunters often use hunting dogs to harass them out of the underbrush. I have seen local 4x4's driving past with a giant black boar strapped to the front bull bars like a trophy, whilst in the back, a trailer full of baying large dogs. Leaving my friend's house late one night, I came across one, ripping open black rubbish sacks in the road. It was easier to just stop and watch him, after ten minutes he obviously decided that he had eaten the best bits. Taking a glance in my direction, he sauntered off into the bushes, leaving a trail of litter all over the road.

I had a favourite walk with the dogs, in the last place that I lived in. Taking their leads off, I would let them roam over the sloping mountainside. Most times they would come back, but on the odd occasion one would not return. After it happened a couple of times I was not too worried, for they knew their way home and would turn up on the doorstep after an hour or so. But on one occasion, my little dog called Bouncy did not return. By the next morning I was worried and went back to the last place I saw him. I never found him, but the earth was all churned up where the giant pigs had obviously been rooting around. I found some dark hairs, so either they had scared him off and he got lost or, they killed him.

We have a lot of big eagles and buzzards that fly overhead looking for food. The eagles seem to like diving down for snakes and hares .The buzzards search out any carrion and there is always something dead in the Campo. Just last week I counted over twenty buzzards flying in low circles right over my head; they have a tremendous wingspan and look majestic. Whilst in flight, their long necks are retracted, giving them a less ominous appearance. Of the smaller birds, the most impressive are the bee eaters. They have gloriously bright colours of red, blues and yellows. To see a whole line of them on a wire is a photographers dream.

CREEPY CRAWLIES AND THINGS THAT BUZZ

There is a down side to living in the campo under a hot sun, especially around here, and that is the enormous amount of flies from late spring right through till the first serious frosts. It is impossible to sit outside after about ten in the morning, without being constantly pestered. If you put up those horrible sticky tape things, they are very effective, but seeing them hanging in your nice living room covered in dead and partly dead, but still buzzing insects is very off-putting. You can also spend all day swotting them with those cheap plastic swots that break after the second thwack, or half kill yourself with cans of spray, that are full of God knows what dangerous chemicals. The heat also brings out all the ticks and fleas, that descend on your loving pets. I had to wash one of my dogs three times in special stuff before he was clean, but that only lasted a week before he was scratching again.

The worst are the garrapatas, nasty looking little buggers that resemble small bug type spiders. They wait around on convenient shrubbery and then attach themselves to any passing animal. They burrow their heads into the skin and suck blood until they resemble a small purple ball. You can grab their bodies close to the skin, twist and pull them off, but if the head remains embedded, then it can lead to an infection. Suggested ways include rubbing alcohol on them to make them pull their heads free, to covering them in butter or Vaseline so they can't breathe. They can spread Mediterranean fever and have also been known to cause the odd human death. An acquaintance of mine, found one embedded in his private parts, he didn't explain how he removed it.

Sand flies can bite animals and is the main reason for so much leishmaniasis in dogs. The dog gets what is basically an immune deficiency problem, and then are open to all sorts of other viruses. It is reckoned that one in four dogs in Andalucía has this problem, which is not un-similar to aids. The normal treatment is a course of injections and tablets for some time after, this does not cure but makes the virus dormant. If untreated the life expectancy is not long.

We have plenty of snakes, vipers are dangerous, but most of the large ones are harmless. I think we have something like 15 varieties in all. One day I was standing in the doorway sipping a cup of tea and looking over the lovely view of Olive groves and mountains, when a big snake dropped against my shoulder. It must have fallen off the roof. My mug of tea went one way and I went the other very smartly. The snake just slid off as if nothing had happened. On another occasion I chased a nasty little viper around the kitchen, whilst it kept hissing at me, finally cornering it under a plastic bucket. In my first year in Spain I was helping a friend clean out an empty swimming pool that was full of mud from a landslip. Suddenly this giant snake appeared and crawled over his shoes. He froze until the moment it had passed over, then jumped out of the pool. I have never seen anyone leap seven feet from a standing start before.

There are also spiders that can hide in places like your bed or socks, and bite you. Often it can cause the leg to swell, and it takes several days of antibiotics to reduce the infection. But that is not as bad as when they lay their eggs under your skin. Two friends of mine have recently received nasty spider bites. It took three weeks of tablets and daily changes of dressings for one of them to recover. Apparently the pain is intense and continuous. Scorpions can give you very painful stings that may have you rushing to the doctor, but they are not fatal, just be careful moving rocks and stones about, or pulling grass up bare handed. A lad who used to live here found one in each of his shoes one morning when he woke up, thank god he saw them before putting his feet in. The caterpillars are also nasty; their fine hairs can cause an allergic reaction and are very bad for dogs who try to sniff them. The processional caterpillar is very fond of pine trees and will go nose to tail in a long line, to find a good one. They then congregate in what looks like a white sack hanging from a branch. Some people spray them with petrol and set light to the sacks to clear the trees. This can also be dangerous because the smoke contains the same fine hairs that you may end up breathing in. Not to mention the fact that in this dry climate you may cause a forest fire. I am told by locals that it is best to fire a bullet through the sack. The shockwave apparently kills them all. There are other large caterpillars that I find in the house from time to time. These have large mandibles and can also cause a reaction from the hair. I was told that they are always in pairs, so often spend an uneasy couple of days looking for the other one. The only good thing I have found about having dog hair on the floor is that somehow they get stuck in it and die. A small amount of dog hair along the bottom of the front door step is also the best preventative for ants getting in, and believe me there are billions out there. It works fantastic, and in all the time I have been here only a few have made it through the defences.

CRUELTY

The next chapter makes me feel sick just writing it, but I have to because it needs to be known. I can't get the photos I have seen, out of my mind. There is a sizable section of the Spanish population that like cruelty to animals. Yes I know we have the same problem with fox hunting and cock and dog fighting in the UK. But after you have read this you may agree that there is something more dark and disturbing about the mentality of people who can do these sorts of things. I am going to leave bullfighting till last, because it almost seems the lesser of these evils.

Every year, a terrified donkey is violently beaten through the streets of Villanueva de la Vera, surrounded by drunk, men. They enjoy beating and kicking, shoving and even dragging it along till it is too weary to move, but then it is forced up and its torture continued. Guns are fired near its ears; alcohol is forced down its throat and the heaviest men in the village attempt to ride it. Only when it is near death, is it taken away to be slaughtered.

Now if you think that is sick how about the bloody Spanish festival which takes place in the streets of Tordesillas. A bull is chased by a horde of young men with pointed sticks that continually stab at it. When the animal is bleeding from dozens of wounds and too weary to run or fight back, its testicles are cut off whilst it is still alive. This spectacle is considered suitable entertainment for the whole family, with parents taking their children to watch. What I can't understand is that once it was made illegal, but in 1999 they started allowing it again.

I love dogs, so this next one really makes me angry. The Galgo is a Spanish Greyhound used by hunters in Spain. At the end of the hunting season it is tradition to kill them very slowly with a torturous death. The ways this is done vary from stringing them up by the neck from a tree, setting them on fire whilst they are alive, wedging their mouths open so they can't eat or drink or dragging them along behind their trucks. Some are thrown down wells, and the lucky ones are just shot. I have to say I have never seen this happening, but if I did, I would not be responsible for my actions, prison sentence or not. This tradition is not an isolated incident; some 50,000 dogs are reportedly meeting these fates every year.

Bullfighting is the most high profile form of animal torture in Spain. It has always been argued that should it be banned, then a big part of Spanish culture would be lost. It is alleged that bullfighters try to elicit inspiration and art from their bloody work, and an emotional connection with the crowd transmitted, through the animal. They say the bull receives a quality life up until the end and is revered for its bravery. My Spanish friend says it is about the raw thrill of man against a mighty beast at the zenith of its powers. That it is in the blood of the Spanish, of their fathers and so on back. We all mostly eat meat, and are not so concerned how we got it and if the animal suffered. So what is so wrong with an animal having a chance to fight back, some of the bravest are given the accolade of being allowed to live? Personally I don't agree with him, I have been to a bullfight, I thought that until I did ,it would not be right to criticise it. Out of the six bulls only one died quickly from the supposed killing thrust of the matador between the shoulder blades, deep into the heart. The others needed several stabs and this was only after they had been worn down by Picadors on a padded horse and had Varas (lances) thrust into its body, as well as Bandaerillas (colourful harpoons). The last one spewed pints of blood all over the sandy floor and took ten minutes to die. I did not even find the pageantry to be spectacular. If anything the whole event felt sordid, as if deep down everyone was exorcising their demons, by being cruel under the disguise of entertainment.

INFORMATION, NOISE AND TELLING THE TRUTH

What no Posters?

The Spanish around here at least are just no good at informing you of anything that is imminent. Even when posters do go up I have noticed that they quite often leave the date or time off. It is assumed that as in previous years the event will take place on the same day and time. I have lost count of the number of events that have passed before I hear anything about it. You can be sure that with such things as local fiestas there will be a booklet ,which is 90% adverts for local bars and restaurants, but these are only obtainable if you know where and when to go and get one. Music events are better as the group involved are keen to publicise.

But it is not the local events that are a real problem, that is reserved for changes in the law. Even the local Abogados (Solicitors), are not always aware of changes, which may seriously affect you. Recently the government put in a new legislation requiring all foreigners to register all of their earnings and properties, including those abroad. Fair enough, I have no problem with that, you must abide by the rules of the country you live in. What gets me is that they didn't inform anyone, you are left to find out for yourself. I suppose that by word of mouth you would eventually get to hear about it. My friend had to ask his solicitor to phone up and enquire three times before it was confirmed. Now the fines for not complying are horrendous, apparently in some cases as much as 30,000 euros. Like I have heard someone say, "The first thing you will know about a new law, is when the fine drops on the mat."

The Spanish love loud

Did you know that Spain was recently voted the second noisiest country in the world; I think the Japanese came first. This is based on decibels in some of the big cities. If you go into most bars in Spain, you will be surrounded by wall tiles that bounce every bit of noise back at you. It only takes a few people discussing their day to actually reach a level that hurts the ears. At this point I have to explain how the Spanish discuss things around here. Firstly someone says something, but before he finishes someone else has joined in trying to talk over the top. They are joined by another and so on, until everyone is talking and no one is really listening. If you watch discussions on Spanish TV it is almost as bad. Not only that but it sounds more like a full on argument, because each point has to be emphasised a little louder than the last. So everything builds to a crescendo. If this is going on with more than one group of people in the same confined space then it is deafening. If you could manage to ask them why they were arguing, they would most likely look at you in surprise and explain that they were having a perfectly amicable conversation. The Spanish are definitely more passionate than the British, they can have a full blown argument and then carry on, whilst we would harbour a simmering resentment for days. Not that the Spanish make friends afterwards, but they shrug and move on to the next situation.

Talking of noise never stay overnight in a hotel that is anywhere near the centre or main roads of a big town or city. The sheer volume of passing traffic during the day is bad enough; they have never really grasped the concept of sound proofing. But it is at night when you want to get to sleep that the fun begins. Firstly if it is summer then you are already extremely warm and may wish to have the window open. Not that it matters because it is not much better if they are closed. The Spanish don't particularly like going to bed, at least not to sleep. So there will be all manner of noises through most of the night, radios, drunken shouting and singing, car horn bibbing and flashing neon lights that just happen to be across from your window. When it does finally start to settle down, the dust carts come around, clashing and bashing bags of empty bottles from all the bars and restaurants. The sound carries, so don't think just because they have finished your street that it will then be quiet. Next they will be around the side or back of the building, then in neighbouring streets. It seems to go on forever. For a short time all is calm, and then you get the early risers who have to open up establishments or just get to work first. They happily walk past talking and laughing loudly. This is followed by the students in the hotel bashing their over large stuffed rucksacks against your door and speaking loudly in some foreign accent as they head for the bus station to continue their backpacking adventure. Then your phone rings and it is the alarm call you innocently pre-arranged the night before. And so starts another day as you shamble down to breakfast, before the morning rush hour really starts upping the decibels. Talking of breakfast, whoever decided that it should be a stale bread roll, one little tub of margarine and one of marmalade and a cup of over milky coffee? What happened to the good old fry-up? Actually one local bar does a reasonable British breakfast after someone went in and showed them how to do it. But only two complaints, their eggs are too runny and under fried and they still can't do good toast, it is more like soggy fried bread, but at least they are trying.

Old cave houses in the Benamaurel cliffs. Originally every cave was like this. Entrance for safety reasons was only down the chimney for these particular examples. One was the local prison with fine views of what you were missing whilst being incarcerated.

DO YOU CHANGE?

What have I learnt about my adopted new country in the 10 years I have been here? Firstly, that there is always other ways of doing things. Just because I spent the first fifty years of my life in a certain way, assured of, and expecting results conforming to a certain pattern of behaviour, doesn't mean that I can expect the same here. Slowly, and I have to admit with a degree of reluctance, I am adjusting to doing everything, in what still appears to me to be a convoluted manner. But heck if it works for them, with a lot of effort it may eventually work for me. I am not against change, it is healthy in moderation, but all at once and full in your face, takes energy I am not sure I have reserves of. I think deep down I am a pipe and slippers man. Warm fire and good English home cooking, with a big cup of tea. Sitting in a tile covered echo filled bar sipping freezing, fizzy lager (It is definitely not beer) and eating slices of chorizo may not be totally unpleasant, but it's not the same, even if it is nice and hot outside. Don't get me wrong, I am not packing up and moving home, I'm here for the long haul, literally. For a start if I sold my 18 room cave system with enough land to build six football pitches, it would not give me enough capital to buy a one roomed flat on the tenth floor of a grey block in Croydon. (Sorry if you love Croydon)

I have to honestly say that the last ten years have been the most eventful years of my life. Strange, sometimes very stressful and it has completely wrecked me physically. But on the other hand I would not swop it for anything else. God knows what I would have been doing if I had stayed in England. Most likely I would have suffered the teaching job, till I was in line for putting out to pasture with a pension and then what? I would have been too old to contemplate moving abroad, I only wish I had done it ten years earlier than I did anyway. Most likely I would be trying to run a bed and breakfast in Norfolk. It does worry me that living out here on my own could prove decidedly more difficult as the years go past; the Campo is not the place for a crusty old man. Mind you, having said that, there are a lot of very old Spanish men, who are tottering around with their hoes over their shoulders, and not looking totally worn out yet.

I know that many of the experiences I have had out here, would never have occurred back in England. If pitting myself against the problems has made me a better person or more fulfilled, it is impossible to calculate. I still feel like a nervous kid inside, and still waiting for the time my brain can be as mature as my body.

I hope you enjoyed this book? I doubt that you agreed with me on many things, we all see situations differently. It was not my intention to pour scorn on the local people of Andalucía, or Spain in general. Most things were said with humour in mind. I am quite prepared to be proved wrong, on any of my comments (except those on animal cruelty). Sometimes you don't even know how you feel about a subject, till you sit down and start writing about it. If you have managed to read the whole manuscript, then I thank you, and I hope there were a few laughs in it for you.

END (well almost)

AFTERTHOUGHTS

These are odds and ends that did not find their way into the main body of the book but for reasons such as promising friends that I would include their contribution, or because it just did not sit happily in any part, or had absolutely nothing to do with grumpy in Spain. So consider this an extra booklet of oddments.

This book was written in one month, from start to finish. The inspiration came from the National Novel Writing Month web site, that challenged want to be authors, to write a novel in thirty days. The worst part was the climbing graph that showed you if you were ahead or slipping behind. Talk about pressure, but it worked. I need that spur of something pushing me, otherwise it would have been written, but not for another year or so. It is like when you go to classes, you are aware that you have to do your homework, but the moment you don't go, then the study goes out of the window. NaNoWriMo as they liked to be referred to sponsor young writer's initiatives and give a lot of support during your month of typing or scribbling furiously. The problem is that if you have to go out for the day, you have two alternatives, either stay up till the early hours doing the required number of daily words, or do twice as many the next day. Miss two days and it really starts to build up. You start to become very un-sociable, declining invitations, ignoring the telephone and even forgetting to walk the dogs. Anyway it all becomes very addictive and I am already starting to consider what the next book will be about, which I think will be on Art, or may be a science fiction story, or thriller, or...

It has since taken me another year to actual try and proof this book, get the cover and art work done and get it out for publication.

THE BRITISH MEETING PLACE

The art of car booting especially in winter is not exactly pleasant. Even here in Spain it means being up at five am, and believe me although I am near the Mediterranean, I am high up and it's still, scrape ice off car windows time. As I sell my paintings, I can't leave them in the car overnight, so have to stagger back and forth numerous times to load up. Then it's off to some god forsaken school playground of transport parking area before setting up your metal stall that sticks to your fingers with the cold. Then you huddle with other idiots, discussing why you bother, as last week you only made 25 euro and some of that had to go on the stall fee. Even at that time in the morning you are beset by individuals who want to see what bargains you have in the back of the van. Some have their own stalls and want to buy cheap off you and sell for a higher price later in the day, when the punters start coming. They can be very intrusive and you really have to watch them closely, the eastern Europeans will be in your car sifting through everything before you know it. When one or two of them get together it is really difficult to keep an eye on your stuff. They wave things around asking how much and then start arguing about it being too expensive. Luckily with painting they are not that interested, but the new car booters, with all their emptied house objects are besieged. I found when I used to take other junk, that the best method was to not put anything out until at least 8.30, just set the empty stall up to reserve your spot, then lock the car and go and have a hot coffee or two in the local café. I found it very hard selling my paintings at car boots fairs; everyone is geared up psychologically to buy really cheaply, unlike a gallery where they expect to pay far higher. It is ridiculous because I could sell the same painting for 20euro or 200euro just depending on where I display it. Mind you at least I stand a better chance at the car boot; I'm not that good an artist. Actually the main problem is the weather. If it is too hot and sunny the pictures sweat and you get stain marks under the glass on the card mounts. If it is wet then everything gets damp and you have to pack away. If it is windy then everything blows about, that you have carefully hung on your home made display stand. When one of the frequently sudden gusts happen, two or three frames go flying and there is the sickening sound of breaking glass. At that point you also pack everything back in the car and go and have a beer or two in the local bar. On rare occasions the weather is just perfect, warm, no wind and just a bit overcast. Then you just pray for a few customers. What you normally get is all your friends coming for a chat, one after another and blocking the front of your stall from the view of any possible prospective buyers. I also tend to wander and end up spending far more than I make, by buying homemade grub and useless items that seemed a bargain at the time. Just looking round you get to recognize certain items that go around and around. Different stall holders buy off each other and a pair of shoes, old wash stands or model train for example can appear each week on a different stall. It's fun to ask questions like, are these yours? Then you get a bullshit story about how they were purchased new but just didn't quite fit, but are a real bargain. If you have nothing better to do, it can be fun having a stall, and the real pro' make a living from going around several car boots during the week. But for me, I will only do it from time to time now, when I have a lot of paintings and no more wall space.

Thinking too deep

It is a strange phenomenon that no matter how good ones life is, we just have to complain about something. When things do get worse, we look back on when it wasn't, and wonder why we complained then. When things are going really well, we say that it can't last, and when it's bad, that we never have any luck. What if we turned things around so that we only ever mention how great things are, even when they are not, just referring to them as good learning opportunities? In good times we could say, "I was glad things were a bit awkward before, as it so makes me appreciate the present. Life is fantastic, and I don't need luck, I'm doing fine." Mind you this approach takes a lot of effort, "Nah! Think I will keep being grumpy and complaining.

Being tall and living in a cave is not a good combination. I remember once thinking it would be good to live on a narrow boat, but the same problem would have occurred. At least in a cave it is normally only the doorways that cause the problem. Most of the rooms are reasonably high. I used to be 6ft 2inches, but after years of bending to kitchen surfaces, drawers and sinks that were built for people somewhat shorter, I have shrunk or more to the point, round shoulders, bad back and sciatica. I also suffer from continuous scabs on the top of my head. Just as one heals up I forget to duck, and bang into another frame. Actually my body is quite short; it's my legs that are long. I know most women would like legs that go on forever, but believe me they can be a nightmare. I ruined my knees being too enthusiastic in my younger years, and running a hundred miles a week on roads, so that I could take part in marathons. The prospect of any long coach ride, plane journey or going to the theatre or cinema is not a pleasurable one. Who designed the spaces between rows, were they midgets or have masochistic intentions. It's hard eating your in-flight plastic wrapped meal, whilst your knees are up around your ears.

The years do pass more quickly as we get older, and I have to admit that the subject of mortality does cross the old brain box from time to time. An old friend turned up at my cave house one day, he is seventy two and his partner is a lady, so I won't mention her age. They are both retired but the interesting thing was that they turned up on a large powerful motorbike, having driven from England. They had already driven all over America on a couple of occasions and visited Germany for a large motor bike rally. They have also done up a narrow boat, on which they spend part of the year and he has not so long ago cycled across parts of Europe. I already feel ancient and I haven't yet reached the age bracket that they have done all this in. Another friend tells me that he attends Yoga classes at which a venerable old lady limped in and joined, a few months ago. She doesn't need the sticks now and can sit cross legged with everyone else. So I need to keep telling myself that I only have one life (As far as I know) and shouldn't waste a minute of it. The time you start feeling sorry for yourself, stop, then go and do something interesting. Invent it there and then if you have to.

Just a little personal ranting.

It is something I still don't understand about the human race, why do we follow fashion so avidly? I don't just mean clothes and hairstyles but, attitudes and actions.

I don't think my next comments are sexist, but if so I apologies in advance, even though there is a degree of truth in it. All the Spanish women under forty over here look the same, there I've said it. Upper calf length boots, tight jeans, leather type jackets and more or less the same long hairstyle. And ladies, if you do have a generous sized posterior, please don't wear tight highly coloured jogging pants. I know in the animal and particularly bird world it pays to have a very visible and colourful arse, but there are limits. And what is it with shoulder tattoos, ankle bracelets and over exposure of cleavages?

We men are not immune; more or less all of us adopt the bald thug look, as soon as our hair starts thinning. It would not be so bad if we actually looked like Yul Brinner, but most end up with the Football hooligan image.

The rubric cube came and went, Sudoku ruled for a while, computer games sell millions of copies so that the young and not so young, can waste half their lives digitally killing each other. And while I am ranting, what is the fascination in watching soaps about warring families, when people would hate it, if it happened to them. As for such programmes based on minor celebrities eating worms or trying to dance or sing, just don't get me started, sometimes I just despair. It is now the age of staring at a small square tablet in our palms.

What happened to individuality, or did it never ever exist.

Cleaning and cooking

Being a bachelor has some advantages, for a start you don't get nagged, can do what you want when you want, and leave all the nasty important jobs till you really can't cope without fixing it. The best part is the house does not have to be spotless. It even helps to appear to visitors, as if you can't really cope, then you get the sympathy vote and offers of help from female friends. As long as you are not actually dirty and smelly, you can present quite a challenge to some members of the opposite sex.

Being interested in creative things such as writing, art and music I have always found, such chores as, cleaning and particularly ironing, not only a complete waste of time, but look on people who enjoy doing it, as sad souls with little point to their lives. Come on, we only have eighty or ninety years, and you want to waste a sizable portion of it dusting? The dust only comes back; the sheets are creased within two minutes of you getting into bed, and who is going to notice your underpants have been ironed, ok, only if you are lucky.

Talking of sex which we weren't, when it gets stale in a relationship, you are generally advised to spice it up by changing the rules, play the game a different way. I do the same when I really have to clean the house, thanks to four dogs and two cats leaving hair everywhere. To prevent boredom setting in after five minutes I started inventing little games. The first was easy; I just did the one hour blitz. Only one rule, you do everything as fast as you possibly can, just like a speeded up film. The dust didn't even have time to hit the floor. Doing it like a dervish, at times I would be washing up cups with one hand, whilst I cleaned the window with the other. It was amazing how much I got done. When that game got tedious I did the Sergeant Major routine, bit masochistic, but I pretended that I was in the army and doing fatigues with a burly officer shouting at me. Weird I know, but it worked for a while. In the end my dislike for authority got to me, and I gave him the proverbial gesture. Then we had the five things in each room. One thing could be something quick, like picking up the books on the floor or long, like actually having to sweep, hoover and wash the floor. That game got reduced to 4 then 3 then 2 jobs in each room. The next game was called, going home. It was based on the simple theory that everything from a bit of dust to a pile of clothes in the house, had a home to go to. I had a big box and would walk from room to room collecting and returning things to their homes. This actually lasted quite a time, subconsciously just as we like to get home, I felt good that everything was safely back where it should be. One of the latest games has been more long term and subtle. The motto was "Never leave a room in a worse state than when you entered it." The results are not obvious but over a period of time it has an effect. The best part is that it does not feel like you are doing housework.

I'm not much interested in cooking. My rule is that for an ordinary meal five minutes is long enough, and for the special occasion fifteen minutes. Mind you I don't mind others taking as long as they want to cook me something, as long as I don't have to sit and wait for it. I once had a meal cooked for me by a friend, it took him over four hours, he downed two bottles of wine and got very drunk whilst doing it, and I ended up with a plate of olives. What is the sense of spending hours preparing something, to watch people shove it down their throats in ten minutes? I am going to be a bit distasteful now, but all those carefully combined flavours, and endless preparation, all get mulched in a mouth, with a portion of saliva, and end up in a sloppy mess of acid in your stomach within seconds. It is not that I don't like food, on the contrary, it is just all the fuss made over it, these endless cooking programmes, where the contestants argue over whose pudding has risen highest.

The death of creativity

I have never been much good at adapting to modern gadgets. Except for odd occasions before I run over them, put them in the washing machine or purposely leave them in some obscure place, I have never really had much to do with mobile phones. I quite like not being got-at-able. The smart phone is completely beyond my comprehension, a bit like one armed bandit machines with all those flashing lights and too many decisions to make.

My chief moan is about the proliferation of people of all ages that have forgotten that real face to face social interaction is still possible. The symbol for this period in our history will be a cut-out of someone staring at their hand which holds a small rectangular pad.

Last week I was served in a local convenience store by a young woman who expertly added up my bill, flipped open the plastic carrier (not easy) and packed all my goods, using just one hand. The whole process was done in mute silence whilst she listened intently to something or someone on her phone that was clamped to her ear. I was tempted to ask her if she needed help levering it off with my penknife, but thought better of it.

Seeing couples out for a romantic meal in a nice restaurant, spending half the time checking their e-mails, is just plain sad. On a similar note, most of the restaurants here in this part of Spain have giant TV screens. Last year a group of us booked a nice table and all sat down preparing to have a good chat and a tasty meal. The first thing the waiter did was to switch on the giant screen next to us and offer the second half of a match between Real Madrid and Barcelona. Now I don't mind watching a bit of football when I really haven't got anything better to do, but now was not the time. He was surprised when we insisted on turning it off, despite a groan from the Spanish man in the corner who obviously didn't fancy talking to his wife for the next hour. Anyway we outnumbered the other diners and the place needed our money.

Bits

This tiny pueblo that I live in is a really strange place, there are so few of us here, but it has its fair share of unusual events. For some reason it has attracted people of an artistic nature. One of these is prone to creating modern conceptual environments. His latest idea was to convince my neighbour to dress up as a Red Indian and stalk around the neighbourhood whilst he took photos of him. Every few seconds my friend had to freeze so that the photo would have some sort of time lapse effect. This was all done in a local quarry and at night. Added to this was the fact that a laser light was being played around him crating strange ghost figures on the photo. Actually the results which were displayed at an exhibition in the nearby town were quite impressive. However the really funny thing was that my friend then proceeded to prowl around an unsuspecting neighbours cave house in the dark, still dressed as a red Indian in full war paint and waving a tomahawk, whilst shouting things like "White man get off of my land." The neighbours reply to his wife was along the lines of "Fuck me, I'm seeing things I've just spotted a Red Indian in the middle of Spain. A few days later they met again only this time my friend had a cowboy hat on and was wearing a deerskin shirt. The neighbours comment was this time something along the lines of, "can't you make your mind up, and are you a cowboy now?"

Today is the 28th November 2015 and it is my birthday. I have spent the last two hours cleaning out dog kennels at the local dog rescue centre, on my own. They were barking a lot so I started singing, "Happy birthday to me" at the top of my voice. It actually worked and they all shut up. I have noticed this phenomenon before, when I start singing and playing my guitar, my dogs at home all go to sleep. Or is that more a comment on my boring singing abilities. After two hours I staggered of to a bar to celebrate with a beer on my birthday. Sitting there all on my own, I got into one of those reflective states where you question what the hell you are doing with your life, and how did I come to end up here? Now I don't want you to think that I am a Billy no mates. Earlier in the day three good friends had called around with presents, cake and even sandwiches, all I had to do was put the kettle on. However for the sake of dramatic effect, there I was sitting supping my lonely half pint and staring at the little plate of tapa which consisted of one lump of indistinguishable meat and a slice of dry bread. I started thinking about what led me to come out here and then to wonder why the other fourteen neighbours who moved from other countries, but mostly Brits also came to end up in this lonely little part of Andalucía.

I am fairy sure I ran away from Britain, not because I had robbed a bank , but because, life demanded I do something drastic before I got any older. Admittedly my partner had died the year before and the house held a lot of memories, but just moving to another part of the UK, would more or less continue a similar existence. At my age this was the last opportunity to really change things whilst I was still fairly fit and young enough to cope. Looking back it was the best move I have ever made, and in a strange way makes sense of my life, but I can't really explain that.

My direct neighbours, the guy who dressed up as an Indian, have been over here for at least fourteen years; they came with rucksacks on their backs and never returned to England. They roamed around Spain, living a bohemian existence in all manner of situations, including living in a tent for quite a while. This was nothing new as for many years they had lived in the Welsh countryside in an old farmhouse and without any transport.

A Dutch friend further down the lane came because the wet climate of Holland did not agree with her body. At first she only came for parts of the year, driving down with her dogs and cats in the back of the van, funny thing was that every time she turned up it started raining here as well.

John, the artist with the laser light, tells of tales of when he lived in Shetland and it was so cold and wet, with full on storms that you just didn't go out for days. I can see why he chose to come here.

Pete had owned a cave house near here for years but only visited infrequently. Having found little work in England, he moved out permanently and his first task was to haul me off the ground and cart me to hospital with my broken leg. Pete is good with computers and electronic gadgets. He set something up in his old mum's house in England so that he could keep a check on her whilst living in Spain. Apparently it looked like a cigarette box that registered every time she walked past it. I am not sure if I am making part of this up, but I think it scared the wits out of her when it suddenly said "Hello Mother, how are you.". His latest plan is to rig up an extremely big and expensive telescope that he has, to the internet, so that people across the world can control it via their computers, for a small payment. The sky around here is absolutely full of stars on a clear night, with no pollution or artificial lighting.

There are three of us who are artists and all named john. I have already mentioned Laser John ,but Juan, who is Spanish, works in Madrid but comes down to his house here quite often. He is a real lothario, although the years are starting to catch up with him, he is good looking, I have to say a bit full of his own importance, but very interesting. He always seems to appear with a new much younger lady on his arm, mostly adult students from his art classes in the city. His old place here is full of contemporary art, the floors are covered in abstract mosaics and he is often out and about in the campo creating art installations. I came home one day to see the abandoned and ruined school house on the hill adorned with long flowing coloured banners streaming out from every window and a semi clothed female with equally long flowing hair popping out of various windows whilst Juan clicked furiously with his camera. With Laser John and Juan both producing creative modern art I feel quite boring knocking out, realistic landscapes.

TIME

Time is very different out here, you go far more by the position of the sun and the feel of the time, at least I do. I don't own a wrist watch or alarm clock, there is little need. The dogs wake me up at approximately the same time each morning. Usually, by making loud grumpy yawns, just outside my bedroom door, if that does not work I get a mock fight. Eating is something that happens when I get hungry; when busy I have been known not to eat anything all day. However that is balanced with the days when I always seem to be looking in the fridge for something to nibble. It may be an unhealthy lifestyle, but I'm still here, I think.

I can lose four or five hours just writing, and apart from a stiff backside, would hardly realise how time has flown. But waiting in a bus terminal for four hours is really boring, unless I take pen and pad with me. Then I come up with all sorts of weird ideas about what is going on around. You should try looking at someone interesting, then imagine where they live and what their life is all about.

I like sleeping; least I did till my body started seriously complaining about the abuse I had put it through over the years. It is kind of scary that we spend seven or so hours each twenty four, totally unconscious. The world goes on around us and we haven't a clue what is happening. So in a life of 85 years we spend something like 744,000 hours, or about 31 years totally out of it. Don't hold me to these figures, my maths is crap, but more or less it is one third of our lives. Add on to that a statistic that says that the average person watches TV for 4 hours a day, so that's 1,460 hours a year ,so let's say they seriously start watching TV at a conservative ten years old (probably more like three) so 75 times 1460 equals 109,550 hours or 45 days plus? Seems an awful lot of time to waste, I could do with some of those back, now that I am getting older.

Have you ever worked at night and slept in the day, it takes a bit of getting used too. It is as if you inhabit another planet from most other people. The world suddenly becomes quite empty, especially if you work outdoors. At first you don't sleep your full quota during the day, for fear of missing something. Out here in the middle of nowhere, I often stay up all night if the muse takes me, especially if there is nothing important to do the next day. Confuses the hell out of the dogs, which lay about groaning as to why I haven't turned the lights off and gone to bed.

Confusion

Why are some people so infuriatingly organised? They have a place for everything and everything in its place. If they need to find the receipt for petrol that they purchased six months ago, they know exactly where to find it. Me, I have enough trouble making sure I have clean underpants for the next day. I had trouble when I was a full time teacher, everyone else had their lesson plans all nicely in order in folders, I did the lesson first then wrote up what I did after, at least that way it was more or less accurate. Unfortunately then I would stuff them in a drawer and not be able to find them when asked by school inspectors, so had to invent them all over again. My little office now is overrun with scribbled bits of paper, Cd's that have lost their sleeves, half read books, bits of computer accessories and the odd musical instrument. Somewhere amongst it all is also a cat or two. Every time I get an idea it gets put on a separate piece, so now I have hundreds of the sheets, stuck in all corners and in no particular order. I am also so much in a hurry that when I come to re-read the stuff I can't always make out what the heck I was talking about. I am not lazy, most days I work quite hard, but when I look around nothing seems to have been done. I hardly ever waste time watching TV, can't sit through a whole film in one go, without thinking I need to go and do something useful. Yet everyone else seems far more on top of their game and organised than me.

In Memory of Bette

Recently a long-time friend died, she was for a time my guiding mentor when I was a teacher. This little story is in memory of her. Once she was kind enough to look after my dog for a couple of days, a few years back. She took it for nice long walks and all was hunky dory until she stepped into a hidden hole and landed up to her armpits in stinging nettles. My dog being, more knowledgeable about his regular route, stood looking down from the rim and wondering why my friend was making howling sounds, which made no sense even in dog language. To be fair it was getting dark so Bette had an excuse for falling into the cunningly constructed bear pit. Shouting for help and waving the slowly dimming torch beam into the night sky, she was lucky to attract a couple of people who also liked marching about in the countryside in the dark. They hauled her out and escorted her back to my place, where she sought solace in a large bucket of icy water. Now the moral of this tale is to never laugh at others misfortunes. Some months after, I was happily walking the dog and reading a particularly interesting article in the running magazine I had with me. Every so often I glanced up to check I was still shuffling more or less down the centre of the path. Now I can't confirm that it was the same hole as the one Bette fell in, but the stinging nettles it contained, had much the same effect on me.

Religion in Spain

Religion has been a big part of Spanish history. I am not going to get into this subject because it is far too emotive, but feel I need to state my opinion. Times are changing, if you go to the local church here on a Sunday, all you will see are mostly old ladies. New Spain does not appear on the surface to be the fierce Catholic country that it once was. But if it is a religious holiday, suddenly everyone turns out to follow the cross or religious sculpture as it is carried around the town. I am not sure whether this is because they like to keep their traditions alive or because they still have a strong faith. There is one parade where the final act is for everyone to fight and scrabble to re-enter the church with their particular icon. I get the impression people turn up to enjoy the spectacle, rather than to honour the Saint in question. I have to admit that the slow solemn night time processions with torchlight and emotive music, does have an effect on your senses, but it is more about the inner emotions of man than any religious fervour. The matter of faith is an individual thing, I am not trying to denigrate it, it's just on a personal level I'm not sure what I believe about the unfathomable. I think if everyone leads a good, honest and caring life there would be no need for religion. Anyway I will await my judgement, if there is to be one.

.

OK that's it, I admit I kind of lost focus and it ended up as just random thoughts, but what do you expect, having written it all in 30 days, you try it. One day I will manage to do a better job of recording my experiences over here, but as they haven't finished yet, I can wait. Since moving to Spain writing has become my passion, along with playing music and painting (Art not walls) I have managed to write eight books, which can be found on Amazon as paperbacks and on Kindle as digital downloads.

Take care and have a good life

John

Other books by John moody:

The Art of Stupidity

Unlikely Bonding

The Old tub Gooseberry

Grumpy in Spain

Private Thoughts and Desires

Dog stories and hairy tails

The Painter (short story compilation)

The Collector of life (under a pen name)

Write, Upload, Sell (How to do it book)

Info at mooinespana@yahoo.co.uk

ABOUT THE AUTHOR

John Moody was born in Sheffield, Yorkshire in 1948, but grew up in Somerset and Hertfordshire. He was not much good at anything but drawing, so he became an Art teacher, although intermittent spells at trying to become a full time artist, met with varied success and failure.

Most of his adult life ,he has played music in a variety of bands, enjoying it greatly, but again with little success, good bands wouldn't have him.

Having retired to Spain and now living in a Cave house, he suddenly got the idea that he could write books. If you have reached this paragraph without skipping all the others,

you deserve a medal.

Printed in Great Britain
by Amazon